P9-ASJ-848

Kitchen Living

Kitchen Living

contemporary ideas for
the heart of the home

Elizabeth Hilliard

with special photography by **Caroline Arber**

Kyle Cathie Ltd

For my family and friends, who make kitchen living such a pleasure

This edition first published in Great Britain, 2000 by

Kyle Cathie Limited

122 Arlington Road

London NW1 7HP

general.enquiries@kyle-cathie.com

ISBN 1 85626 366 5

Text © 2000 Elizabeth Hilliard

Special Photography © 2000 Caroline Arber

Photography © 2000 Laura Hodgson

Photography © 2000 Francesca Yorke

Photography © 2000 Ray Main

Commissioning Editor: Kate Oldfield

Editor: Eugenie Boyd

Production: Lorraine Baird and Sha Huxtable

Designer: Heidi Baker

Colour repro: Colourscan

Elizabeth Hilliard is hereby identified as the author of

this work in accordance with Section 77 of the

Copyright, Designs and Patents Act 1988

A CIP catalogue record for this title is available from

the British Library

Printed and bound in Singapore by TWP

contents

introduction

KITCHEN LIVING IS TODAY'S WAY OF LIFE. ONCE UPON A TIME THE KITCHEN WAS SOLELY A DOMESTIC OFFICE, A ROOM WHERE THE MESSY AND LABORIOUS BUSINESS OF PREPARING FOOD TOOK PLACE. THEN IT BECAME A BRIGHT, SPARKLING HAVEN IN WHICH THE POST-WAR HOUSEWIFE COULD ADMIRE HER BUILT-IN UNITS AND PREPARE DELICACIES FOR HER MAN'S HOMECOMING. TODAY'S KITCHEN HAS UNDERGONE YET ANOTHER REVOLUTION. IT IS THE CENTRE OF THE HOME, ESPECIALLY A FAMILY HOME. IN THE TRUE SENSE OF THE WORD, IT HAS BECOME THE HOME'S 'LIVING ROOM', THE LIVING KITCHEN.

The living kitchen is where we sit, eat and drink, talk, work and entertain friends. Children play, there is a comfortable chair or a sofa, the telephone has been joined by a television and sound system. Outside there is a terrace with a table and chairs that we use as an extension of the kitchen in fine weather, as if we were living by the Mediterranean. Whether we are country people or confirmed urbanities, we are addicted to kitchen living.

Kitchen living is truly international. It originates in the warm, bustling, garlic-scented farmhouse kitchens of Tuscany and Provence, but its most famous exponents, on opposite sides of the North Atlantic, are probably Martha Stewart and Terence Conran. Both internationally famous and hugely influential, each in their own way has contributed to the revolution, helping to shape the way people decorate, equip and use their kitchens, including the food they cook and eat there. Needless to say, their own kitchens are fabulously decorated centres for kitchen living.

CHAPTER ONE
PLANNING AND STORAGE

KITCHEN LIVING REQUIRES AN IMPRESSIVE AMOUNT OF EQUIPMENT AND FURNITURE TO MAKE IT COMFORTABLE – EVERYTHING FROM THE COFFEE GRINDER TO THE CHAIR BY THE TELEPHONE. HOW TO FIT IT ALL IN WITHOUT BUILDING A NEW HOME? HERE ARE WORDS OF ADVICE ABOUT HAVING IT ALL, FROM SEATING THE ENTIRE FAMILY AND ENTOURAGE AROUND THE TABLE FOR SATURDAY LUNCH, TO ARRANGING YOUR GADGETS SO THAT EVERY LITTLE THING IS EXACTLY WHERE YOU WANT IT WHEN YOU WANT IT.

WELL-PLANNED DETAILS go a long way to making life a pleasure. If you had the chance to create a living kitchen from scratch, what would it include? A cooking area that is a joy to work in with plenty of storage space, of course. A table that can become larger or smaller according to numbers and use. A sofa or other comfortable seating. A place for children to play safely? An open fire or stove, even, to warm those winter evenings? A living kitchen can't have everything. Or can it? Why not, space allowing? And for the kitchen which is neat and small, there are some great space-saving ideas that prove you don't necessarily have to sacrifice atmosphere to practicality.

Whatever the size of your living kitchen you need storage – as much as possible – for kitchen living. Some of it is best built-in, making the most of available space. Free-standing furniture has a part to play, adding interest and character to the room as well as offering storage space. Parts of the room which are often overlooked, such as the upper walls and the ceiling, can also provide storage opportunities, as can portable objects like racks and baskets.

the way
we live now

DOMESTIC LIFE has undergone a revolution in the past century or so – several revolutions in fact. In the first decade of the 20th century a huge number of families either employed a servant (female), or had members who were employed as such. Household gadgets were available, but they were barely labour-saving by our standards, and they did not alter the fact that the servant bore the brunt of the hard work.

Today, it is accepted that domestic labour is a co-operative effort made by all members of the family. The actual distribution of responsibility and work may often lag behind this non-sexist, non-stereotypical ideal, but machinery of all sorts has in any case removed or reduced dramatically the slog involved in servicing a household. In addition, many homes have a wash-kitchen or utility room into which much of this machinery fits. This leaves the kitchen itself free to fulfil its contemporary function as a room for the enjoyment of food – its preparation and eating – as well as, by extension, other companionable activities. The cook of the family is no longer satisfied to slave in an isolated backroom kitchen to which, in any case, the family and visitors will inevitably gravitate.

The way we live now seems so much better, more equable and sociable, more relaxed than in previous generations. Mealtimes are fun, with inspiration for the colourful and flavoursome food we eat coming from across the globe. We simply don't have the time to worry about making a 'good' or 'right' impression on family or friends, even if we thought such an ambition desirable. Anyway, they are probably all living in their kitchens too.

Even when small, our children are (we hope) our friends and we want to enjoy their company, at all times, not only mealtimes, and be involved in their games and activities. Property values mean that a room so little used as a formal dining room is often unviable, and if we do have one it probably sees more service as a home office or storage depot than for meals. We almost don't need a sitting room any more, such is the popularity of the living kitchen.

before you start planning

Before embarking on a plan for your kitchen, get back to the basics. Make a list of who uses the room for what, prioritize these, and invite suggestions for improvements and innovations. Remember, however, that you cannot please everyone; if you are the person who will be using the kitchen most, the most important person to please is you. The pages that follow are designed to help you have the most pleasing kitchen possible.

fitted or unfitted?

WHETHER TO have a kitchen that is fitted or unfitted is often a question that answers itself, either because of your budget or because of the space available for the kitchen's necessary practicalities, namely food preparation and the storage of kit. A fitted kitchen generally makes maximum use of limited space but is more expensive than an unfitted one. Ideally, however, the choice of fitted or unfitted is down to looks and your own preference.

the pros and cons

Some people find the neatness and uniformity of a fitted kitchen oppressive while for others it is the desirably compact and efficient solution. To some, an unfitted kitchen provides the look of a home, with real furniture, while to others it looks scrappy and scruffy. Certain kitchen companies fulfil their clients' fantasies by producing magnificent fitted kitchens that have the homely, embracing look of the idealised rustic farmhouse or Mediterranean kitchen complete with turned oak spindles and yards of dresser-style display

shelving. The real thing, ironically, is entirely unfitted except where the range and the sink are attached to the necessary services.

Many kitchens today are a mixture of fitted and unfitted, and this recipe suits the living kitchen because it offers variety and flexibility. An unfitted kitchen can make a room look larger, because you can see the full extent of the floor under the furniture. Under the sink (which obviously has to be fitted to the wall) you can hang a cheerful curtain if you want to conceal clutter. Replacing fitted wall units with open shelves will increase the sense of space, because you can see the wall behind.

If there is already a fitted kitchen in place, but you don't like it, you may well be able to transform it without great cost by painting, replacing or removing doors, changing or painting tiles and worktops (using specialised paints and preparations), changing knobs and handles, altering the configuration of equipment, cupboards and shelving, and by introducing some colour that is more contemporary and more to your taste.

Fitted kitchens (opposite) usually offer the best use of available space. They come in all styles, including the sleek and modern, as above, and the traditional (below). The latter is in the Shaker style, combining simplicity and elegance with pleasure in the quality of natural materials, mainly wood. The smart, contemporary kitchen above it uses plenty of stainless steel.

Unfitted kitchens (above and left on this page) vary hugely too, from those which use recycled wooden furniture (see more about this in 'The Natural Kitchen' on page 48) to the cool and contemporary. Catering units like these, above, provide rugged, freestanding units and surfaces, while trolleys with castors offer versatility and extra storage. The unfitted island on the left has a toughened glass top and includes a hob, oven, sink and cupboards finished in smooth polished timber.

oven, hob

WHEN PLANNING your kitchen, the three vital elements to position first are the oven, hob and sink, though the fridge is also important, along with the dishwasher and microwave if you have them, and any other electrical equipment (including the washing machine, if this is in the kitchen, and the boiler).

Water, electricity and gas can be piped to and from almost anywhere in a kitchen, so don't feel constrained by the existing arrangement unless you are on a minimal budget, in which case you will have to adapt your ideas to their present positions.

Ideally, the oven should be raised off the ground so that you don't have to stoop to lift heavy weights, and it is important for safety to have somewhere immediately beside it where you can put down a hot pan. The hob needs the same, and also a window or an

Cooking has never been such a pleasure. Hobs (left, above) **such as gas** (lower of the two illustrated) **and halogen** (above) **offer instant responsive heat for every style of cooking. Ovens can be separate, installed at worktop height, or incorporated into a stove like these** (left and right). **Both the ultra-modern stainless steel range with integral hood** (right) **and the classic enamelled Aga** (left) **offer the versatility of two ovens with different functions, though the Aga lacks a grill.**

and sink

extractor fan above. The oven also needs space into which the door(s) can open.

Freestanding ovens can be powered by gas, electricity, oil or solid fuel. They usually include oven, hob, grill and sometimes other devices like griddle or deep-fat fryer. They are generally finished in stainless steel, white, black or brown, though some, like the traditional-looking Aga, are available in a range of colours to match the rest of your kitchen.

The sink can go wherever drainage is possible and is often placed under a window, which is fine if this is not the only window in your kitchen. Where it is, the better option is to put the sink against a back wall so that the table can go near the window where you can enjoy the light, view and fresh air whilst sitting there.

Sinks (right) **come in many shapes and forms to match every style and in sizes varying from the generous (like the vitreous china sinks in the Shaker kitchen below) to the small-is-beautiful to fit into a tight corner or a small galley kitchen. Materials include Corian** (above)**, stainless steel, enamel, copper, ceramic and china.**

kitchen kit

WHETHER YOU are moving house or planning a new kitchen from scratch, spring cleaning or simply fed up with clutter, there comes a time in the life of every kitchen when you need to take a long, hard look at your kit. Excavate the back of cupboards to discover what you already own, and at the same time make a list of dream gadgets that (if you had them) would get almost daily use and make your life easier. Do you have a dusty fondue set you never use, for example, and are you forever going to the shop for fresh bread when a baking machine would save you the trouble and give you hot, organic loaves?

big pieces

Kitchen kit includes the big stuff like the fridge or fridge/freezer and dishwasher, medium-sized pieces like food processor and coffee machine, right down to your favourite corkscrew and potato peeler. They are all important. The big things obviously have to be considered in the early stage of planning the lay-out

of a kitchen; the smallest need an easy-access drawer in which to lie. It is the gadgets of medium size, generally used on the counter top, that pose the greatest challenge.

medium-size gadgets

If you use them almost daily, they should ideally be in a position where they can remain plugged in and ready to use without being heaved about (some are quite heavy). But a row of machines creates exactly the sort of clutter you want to avoid – they look a mess and take up precious space. The ideal solution is to have a cupboard from counter level upwards, just deep enough to house the largest gadget and with plenty of sockets, all the way up. The largest, heaviest items go at the bottom with their accompanying bits and pieces, while the lightest go higher up. They are all plugged in and can be drawn out or taken down easily as required. A sliding door, roller blind or rolling shutter draws across or down to hide them.

A helpful list of possible kitchen kit:

- Fridge
- Freezer
- Dishwasher
- Extractor fan
- Other built-in pieces like an in-sink waste disposal machine
- Clothes washer and drier if these are in the kitchen
- Kettle
- Food processor and collection of blades/bowls
- Toaster
- Yoghurt maker
- Toasted-sandwich maker
- Fizzy-drinks maker
- Deep-fat fryer
- Baking machine
- Blender
- Electric grinder for spices
- Coffee-making kit
- Stalk liquidiser
- Pestle and mortar
- Potato masher
- Corkscrew
- Potato peeler
- Sharp scissors

Choosing your kitchen kit requires firm resolve, so enticing is the range of available styles and specifications. Excavate the backs of cupboards to discover the items you thought you couldn't live without but have happily forgotten. Replace them with a new generation of essentials. When choosing the really big pieces, be realistic about your requirements and be sure that you can get them in through the door.

wiring and lighting

WIRING AND LIGHTING are factors to include at an early stage of planning. They can be altered in an existing kitchen, but it is obviously easier and you have more scope if it is done before any units are fitted.

wiring

Wiring is needed for the following items in a kitchen, besides lighting:

- **Sockets, plenty of them**

- **Electric hob and/or oven**
- **Extractor fan**
- **In-sink waste disposal unit**
- **Built-in equipment like deep-fat frier**

Sockets clearly want to be in positions where equipment like fridge, freezer and dishwasher are fitted. You want at least one socket each side of obstacles like the hob and sink, across which you should not stretch a flex. If you have a cupboard for medium-sized gadgets, it will need plenty.

Consider the list of kit on page 17 and mark each one that you own and which needs electric power. Install more sockets than you think necessary – you may find you use them all.

lighting

Possible types of lighting include:

- **Overhead lighting for cooking area**
- **Baffle lighting (underneath wall-mounted cupboards)**
- **Over cooker (this is often incorporated into an extractor hood)**
- **Over table**
- **General lighting for the whole room**
- **Lighting or sockets for lamps for other activities, eg desk work or computer use**
- **Lighting on any special objects or works of art which decorate your kitchen**
- **Outdoor lighting so that you can see the terrace or garden after dark and use it in summer**

Finally, you may want some of your lighting on a dimmer switch, or switched in more than one place around the room.

Lighting has entered a new era of variety and versatility. The living kitchen requires several different types for the room's different functions. List the activities that take place here and envisage the ideal lighting style for each. Halogen downlighters built into a boxed architrave (opposite) lend sumptuous illumination to the working areas. For eating and/or working at the table consider one of these types: the pendant lamp with opaline glass shade (above left) or classic fisherman's lamp (below left). The many facets of these star-shaped lamps in Moorish style (above right) give a pretty, scattered general light, while these handy labels (below right) keep perfect order at the socket end of operations.

leisure
in the kitchen

THE IDEAL kitchen has a comfortable squashy sofa or armchair where you can curl up with a cup of coffee or glass of wine while waiting for the timer to tell you supper is done or simply to enjoy a few minutes of blissful solitude.

There are plenty of other leisure activities that can and do take place in the kitchen, however, involving all members of the household. Many kitchens have a small television, music system, and even a desk or table for household management and paperwork. This is the area, in a big kitchen, where you might also want a computer, for work, play and access to the internet. If possible, keep TV and music systems off the floor. Compact models will fit on a shelf or wall-bracket, for example.

There are two other aspects to the question of where to put larger equipment such as a television and computer. The first is: do you really have space in the kitchen for them and/or is this the right room in the house for them? If the answer is 'Yes', your second consideration is power. Does this area of the kitchen have sufficient sockets, electrical, television and telephone (for the modem as well as the phone itself), to service your needs? Are they in a suitable place? Scrambling around on the floor amongst an ugly tangle of wires and cable extensions to secure the right connection is a sure source of irritation. It is not generally a big job for an electrician to install several extra sockets provided there is at least one socket there already (and he or she might as well add more in the cooking area, if you need them, while they are in the house).

As for the look of all this equipment – not only does it need storage so that it can be shut away from sight when you are using the room for meals or entertaining, but it also needs protecting from dust and grease. A cupboard or desk with a roller shutter offers one solution, another is a home office unit of the type which looks like a handsome cupboard when the doors are closed – there are now plenty of these on the market. Or if you are employing a joiner for other work in the kitchen, he may be able to make you a desk-cum-cupboard to your own design, making maximum use of the available space. Alternatively, fill one wall with a smart storage system that will house all your music, leisure equipment and accessories and even have room for your cook books.

This Shaker-style dresser (left) stores and displays a beautifully serene and restrained selection of china, chopping boards, boxes and a magnificent wooden bowl. The result looks like a work of art. The more familiar clutter of a living kitchen can be hidden in cupboards like this (below), equipped with a revolving wire shelf and fronted with chicken wire. Drawers (opposite) can be a design feature. These are made of basket (above) inset into sliding wooden frames, or fronted with riveted glass (below).

shelves and drawers

CUPBOARDS PROVIDE only one form of kitchen storage, and one with problems. The front of the cupboard is easily accessible, but not usually the back. This is fine for items that are rarely used, but objects tend to lurk in the recesses of deep cupboards, gathering dust and grease. You hardly use a particular gadget, so you put it at the back; because it's at the back, you are even less likely to use it.

open shelves

Shelves and drawers offer an alternative, and one with better visibility and accessibility. Moreover, by storing your favourite cookware on an open shelf you have the pleasure of looking at its handsome forms. A row of gleaming stainless steel or copper pans is a fine sight. The habit of displaying cookware in this way may have died out as a result of the introduction of aluminium pans which become grey and pitted as they age – not an attractive sight. Modern stainless steel does not have this disadvantage.

pros and cons

Accessibility is an advantage of both shelves and drawers. You can see things at the back, and reach them easily. This, of course, is not such a good idea if the shelves are within reach of small children; save display of your favourite china until they are older. Drawers can be fastened with child-proof catches; sharp knives can be stored at counter level or higher in a block or on a magnetic strip.

There are other disadvantages to storage on shelves. Objects have no protection from grease in the kitchen atmosphere, but this hardly matters if you have a really efficient extractor over the cooker. Also, a jumble of items is revealed as such on an open shelf. If there is a visual theme – all blue and white, for example, or all well-designed, brightly coloured product packaging – this will create an interesting display. If the jumble is just that, better to conceal it in a cupboard. When it comes down to it, kitchens simply cannot do without them.

storing cook and tableware

COOK AND tableware generally fall into two categories – those items you use almost every day and those you don't. Those you do want to be stored close to the place where they are used – ie, close to the cooker or table. Deep, strong drawers are better than cupboards (see previous pages) for cookware. Differing views prevail about storing china and glass for the table. Should it be stored close to the dishwasher or sink, or to the table so that this can quickly and easily be laid for meals?

The solution may lie in the layout of your particular kitchen, but there are other factors to consider. Assuming that the dishwasher and table are not adjacent, would you rather make the extra effort of carrying china between dishwasher and storage, or between storage and table?

Glass has special requirements. It is best kept well away from the steamiest part of the kitchen or it will gather grease and dust. This is true even if you have an extractor fan – the slightest amount will show on glass when barely noticeable on china.

Two more guidelines: keep like with like, and don't forget the possibility of displaying your finest or most interesting pieces as part of the kitchen's decoration. This could involve ranging them along a shelf, or hanging a collection of cookware items from a rack or rail.

Rather more has been crammed onto the white-painted dresser (opposite) **than on the Shaker version on the previous page, but because the china is all carefully chosen (pale, with a few black items) and artfully arranged, the result still manages to look restrained and supremely stylish. Exquisite Chinese gilt-edged ceramic bowls** (right) **are displayed and stored on well-lit shelving exactly in proportion with their size. Cookware** (below) **looks handsome ranged on open shelves.**

storing food

IT IS most kitchen-dwellers' dream to have a larder – a cupboard or small room dedicated to the cool storage of foodstuffs. The larder may have been associated with grand houses in the past, but it has proved to be a useful and popular kitchen adjunct in the present.

Today, though, even a spacious home rarely has a whole room dedicated to the purpose. A cupboard is the more likely option, either built in or as a freestanding separate entity. Make sure you have plenty of shelving for storage, a cool surface provided by a marble or slate slab, and a cool, low-humidity atmosphere. The latter can be achieved naturally in temperate climates with an air vent exiting on the cool side of the house, or artificially with heat-exchange controls similar to those in a refrigerator.

Food in the kitchen generally falls into several categories:

- FRESH foods, including dairy produce, fruit and vegetables
- DRY foods such as rice and pasta
- MOIST foods such as bread and cake
- PRESERVED foods – canned and frozen
- FLAVOURINGS such as herbs, spices, sauces, and oils and vinegars
- PREPARED food waiting to be cooked or eaten.

fresh and dry

Fresh foods include those kept in the fridge, those on display such as fruit, and others which need darkness and cool, fresh air to keep them in good condition, like potatoes and onions. Keep the latter in a well-aired cupboard or in baskets or mesh-bottomed drawers, preferably with extra ventilation holes drilled in the sides. Dry foods are often bulky – pasta, flours, cereals and pulses for example – but can be attractive if stored in a row or stack of large clear jars. Moist foods need cool, fairly airtight conditions but are not usually stored in the refrigerator.

cans and flavourings

Foods preserved in cans are not generally attractive, but items like tomatoes, pulses and tuna are invaluable for quick meals and can be stored out of sight. Flavourings need to be quickly and easily reached from the cooker. Many cooks prefer them kept out on narrow shelves or a rack rather than in a cupboard, which can complicate access.

prepared food

The cold slab in the larder proves its worth when it comes to storing prepared food that is waiting to be cooked or eaten – before or after a party, for example. Those of us without the luxury of a larder have to find space in the fridge, the utility room, the garage, the cellar… anywhere sufficiently cool, spacious and secure from animals and small children.

storage tips

The ideal living kitchen has resources for all these types of food within reach of the food preparation area. The cupboard under the sink, for example, traditionally stores cleaning materials. Banish these to the utility room or elsewhere and use it for bulky vegetables. A drawer as deep as a can will store tins of food and you can reach the ones at the back as easily as those at the front. A long narrow space – over a window, across a fireplace or above head height where people sit at the table – will accommodate a shelf for jars of dry foods. Alternatively, have only a little of everything near the cooker and back-up supplies in a cupboard elsewhere – the garage or utility room, perhaps.

The ideal kitchen has a cool larder for storing foods which don't need the chill of the refrigerator, but a magnificent cupboard like this (above) will do the job almost as well. Vegetables keep fresh in ventilated drawers like these (middle right), or drill holes in an existing kitchen drawer. Or use a freestanding item like this vegetable rack (top right). A wall-hung set of small see-through fronted drawers (right) stores and prettily displays dried pulses.

food preparation and waste disposal

IN A FAMILY situation, or if you entertain at home regularly, the preparation of food is likely to be the most frequent and time-consuming activity your kitchen sees apart from the time spent enjoying the resulting meals. The ideal kitchen has a spacious worksurface next to the cooker, sink and dishwasher, at a height that suits you. This may mean having a plinth built under your fitted kitchen units if you are very tall, or having units and doors cut down if you are short. Bear in mind, however, if you are planning to move on sooner rather than later, that this may not suit prospective buyers.

recycling

Food preparation and consumption produces a large amount of waste, some potentially productive (such as vegetable matter if you make compost for your garden), some recyclable (a lot of packaging in most geographic areas), some of it depressingly everlasting (most plastics). In some countries, manufacturers are responsible for recycling, so you could in theory discard all cosmetic packaging at the checkout of your supermarket (and this would make a statement in countries without such legislation). Many supermarkets already act as recycling centres, to their credit.

In your home, recycling takes space and trouble, but it is generally worth it. At the same time, choosing products with little or no packaging saves the time (and fuel) it takes to manufacture and then to unwrap and recycle it.

kitchen bin

In the kitchen, the debate rages about the size and siting of the bin. Should it be built-in and concealed, or freestanding and therefore moveable to the site of the mess? Should it be small and discreet or large and commodious? Each option has its advantages and disadvantages – ask yourself what is most convenient for you and your household, bearing in mind the activities that take place in your kitchen. Perhaps two bins would provide a solution. Or would having an in-sink waste disposal system help?

Contrary to popular belief, egg shells (opposite left) **compost well. Even a small compost bin, in a small garden or on a terrace or balcony, is useful for recycling uncooked waste vegetable matter and other items generated by food preparation, creating home-made compost for your containers. This clever trolley-bin** (above) **has separate compartments for different types of waste under its hinged lid, and a deep drawer below for storing bottles prior to a visit to the bottle bank.**

families

IT IS unusual for a living kitchen not to be host to families with children at some point, and if you have small children of your own it is likely to double as a playroom as its most frequent function after the preparation and consumption of food. People with a separate playroom tend to find that this is abandoned in favour of the kitchen – so much more appealing if that's where mother, father or the nanny is busy – unless the playroom opens directly off the kitchen and the loved one can be seen and heard from there.

art and toys

With a big kitchen this poses few problems. A cupboard or specially imported storage system, preferably, for safety reasons, at the opposite end of the room from the cooking area, is given over to books, toys and art materials, each in a separate container, such as a plastic box or a basket, for easy transportation.

If there is no room in the kitchen for these to be stored, then they should ideally be kept in a room nearby, whence they can easily be brought as required. A kitchen with absolutely no container for errant toys is likely to drive you mad with annoyance, as small children inevitably bring things of interest with them from elsewhere – things you will want to gather together rather than making endless small expeditions to put them away.

kitchenware cupboards

Even with generous provision for children's activities, a small person is going to find the cooking end of the kitchen attractive because adults are active there and, with so many drawers and cupboards to explore, it promises excitement. If you don't want always to be saying 'No!', consider having one cupboard into which children <u>are</u> allowed, containing perhaps your baking and roasting trays or plastic containers or other innocuous (though not necessarily silent) items. Other cupboards and drawers can be fitted with child-proof catches.

using space

USING SPACE successfully is so often a question of scale as much as of organisation. Large furniture and fittings in a small room look as ridiculous as small ones in a huge room and are equally impractical. Moreover, it is easier to plan a small kitchen that is efficient and good-looking than a really large one, for which you may welcome the help of a professional designer or architect in order to make the most of the space without finding the room exhausting to use.

After scale, the next consideration is space management. Consider the list you have made of who uses the room and for what. Would you rather it were otherwise? If so, make a list of the activities you would like to include, and which you would like to exclude (and alternative sites for these). Be realistic. If cooking is only one of several activities, allocate a confined (albeit suitably generous) floorspace for this.

Think about the uses to which the table is put, besides eating, and allocate space for back-up storage for these (probably on shelves or in a cupboard). If you have a television in the room, does its position allow you to be comfortable while watching it (and is there a comfortable chair)? Is the telephone in a convenient position and is there a handy place for paper for messages? What are the things that

cause you little annoyances in the kitchen with its current configuration and what changes would you like to make?

Make a plan of the room and make several copies of this to draw on. Imagine you are seeing this space for the first time, completely empty, without units or furniture, a blank canvas. Now draw your ideas for what should ideally go where onto the plan, redrawing as many times as it takes for you to be satisfied. Give each element and activity as much space as it needs or can be realistically given, with as little overlap as possible. Relax and enjoy this process – planning can be fun.

Think boldly. You may end up with a predictable arrangement but playing with other ideas will help convince you that this is the correct one. You don't want to feel, later, that you missed an opportunity. If the sink is under the window, for example, how about moving it and the food preparation area to a back wall so that the table can be by the window? If the kitchen is very small, how about knocking through to make one much larger room? Or consider moving the kitchen entirely from a tiny room to another (larger) room while the smaller room then becomes a generous larder and utility room.

This neat galley kitchen is designed to take up as little space as possible whilst being practical and convenient for preparing meals. It stands in the corner of a generous living space, which unites all the household's social activities, including cooking.

IT IS usually the case that fitted units give you the maximum storage space and worksurface area within the constraints of a small kitchen. But fitted units can be confined to one or two sides only, depending on the shape of the room, giving an efficient working 'triangle' between sink, cooker and fridge, whilst leaving space for a neat table and at least a couple of chairs.

The most intriguing small kitchens are positively Lilliputian. They fit into a cupboard which you can stand on one side of any other room, complete with sink, rings for cooking, fridge and storage. Various companies make them in varying combinations of contents. Stand one of these in your sitting room or studio and bring new meaning to the term 'living kitchen'.

Boats (and caravans) also offer inspiration for owners of small kitchens. There's no question of a separate dining room, yet in the galley everything that is needed is there, packed with great ingenuity into a small space. On shore, meanwhile, remember that many kitchen machines are available in small or narrow editions, including dishwashers, washing machines and hobs.

A small kitchen does not need to lack style. This handsome mini-kitchen balances rugged exposed brickwork with the glossy grey-speckled surface of polished granite, coloured cupboard fronts and streamlined stainless steel handles.

the small kitchen

With a tiny kitchen in its own room, look beyond its four walls. Does the adjoining room have space for a larger and more comfortable eating area? If so, you have the option of linking these two spaces both practically and visually. Practically, you can open up the two to each other by widening the door, making a large hatch through the wall, or lowering the wall to above counter height (the latter two ideas are likely to be more complicated and expensive if this is a load-bearing wall). Visually, use colour to link the cooking area with the eating area, not just on the walls but also on the floor by continuing the same flooring through the two spaces, and similarly by using the same colour on the ceilings.

It is even more vital in a small kitchen than a large one to look for wasted spaces that could be used for storage. The upper part of walls is often under-used. If you cannot easily reach that far, keep only rarely used items there, or have a small stool or step that is easy to move around and put away when not in use. A rail or rack can be placed across the top of a window and small shelves can be screwed individually onto the wall for storing lightweight, often-used items like herbs and spices.

Wherever possible, store items off your worksurfaces, so that clutter does not gather. Larger items such as a microwave or small grill can be lifted off the worksurface by placing it on a stand, a shelf or a bracket of the type more frequently used for televisions. It may be necessary, though, simply to have a clear-out and edit your possessions. Too much stuff makes a small room look smaller.

All that's needed to accommodate this fabulous stainless steel kitchen is a few metres of wall-space. Within this is packed sink, hob, large oven and full-size fridge/freezer as well as plenty of storage space. Commission a custom-made equivalent and include the equipment to suit you – dishwasher or microwave, perhaps.

the medium-sized kitchen

The owner of this kitchen is a skilled craftswoman-embroiderer whose eye for detail is apparent in every corner. Serene and spacious, the room nonetheless manages to incorporate and conceal the home's boiler (below, third from left) and washing machine (below, far right). This is a dream kitchen in having elegant French windows (main picture opposite) opening on to a terrace and small but verdant city garden.

A MEDIUM-SIZED kitchen is perhaps the easiest to plan and manage, having neither the severe constraints of a small room nor the alarming distances of the large one. It has a cooking area that is compact but not cramped, with plenty of well-lit worksurfaces. It has room for a table that seats at least six and can perhaps be expanded to seat ten for a party. It has a comfortable chair near the telephone or television, or sited so that you have the best view out of the windows when you are sitting in it. In total, it's a pleasure to work in and sit in.

A kitchen of this size offers at least one temptation that is to be avoided. Because it is a generous-sized room, the danger is that one gets carried away and puts too much in it. Certainly, it has greater space for more activities, but if you exercise some restraint you will be rewarded with a room that is serene and spacious as well as being the hub of the home.

Limit cooking equipment and preparation spaces to two walls in an 'L' shape, or at one end of the space, leaving a good part of the room for living in. Have the same practical flooring throughout to unify the different areas, with a rug at the sitting end if you want to soften the floor and introduce a touch of luxury. Plan your lighting so that one area or another can be brightly illuminated when in use while others are dim or dark. Use colour throughout the room, linking cooking and other areas by having accents and accessories such as tiles, table linen, cushions and lampshades, in the same or related colours.

This fabulous kitchen has a preparation/cooking area, dining area and (out of sight behind us) conservatory opening into the garden, all created out of a set of small, dingy rooms in a city semi-basement. The owner wanted the sink under the window, but this was awkward to arrange without spoiling the spaciousness created by the floor going the full length of the room, uninterrupted, and because there is a door in the wall to the right of the window. The solution was radical – a triangular stainless steel sink and draining board was specially made to fit. The result is dramatic – the sink no longer seems utilitarian but more like a piece of sculpture.

the large kitchen

IF YOU have a gloriously large living kitchen you are lucky indeed, a possessor of a luxury of which most of us can only dream. You also have quite a job on your hands deciding what will go where. Bear in mind the source of daylight, access into the room and routes through it to other spaces when you are planning how to fit the different elements of the room together like a jigsaw. A professional designer or architect could assist with ideas and technical expertise, and also help you complete the project within your budget.

Your cooking area wants to have a clearly defined floorspace, as do the eating and leisure areas. A peninsular or island unit will help define the food preparation and cooking section and prevent it becoming exhaustively huge. A peninsular unit is one which sticks out from the wall; an island stands alone and can be fixed or moveable. If fixed, it can be larger and more commodious, and also have a water supply. This could lead to the main sink or to a small sink for washing vegetables, for example, or making tea and coffee.

If your budget matches the size of the room, or is at all generous, you will be in a position to consider having some really magnificent equipment in your kitchen, such as a 'professional' stainless steel stove with five or six gas rings and two big electric ovens or one huge one.

This enormous country kitchen has the floor area of many a small urban apartment. It has a huge cooking and eating area (left), with copious cupboards and a welcoming table decked in a bright cloth, while glass-paned doors open into the garden (above). Undoubtedly the living kitchen of many people's dreams . . .

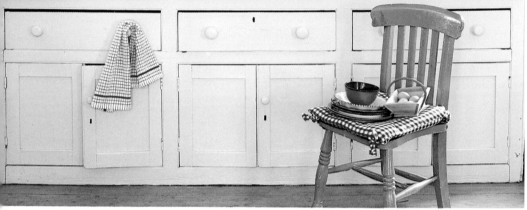

The clutter on the dresser (above) in this same kitchen is prevented from looking a mess by the choice of a blue/yellow/white theme. The sitting area of this spacious room (opposite) has an open fire and a fine display of the children's artwork.

You might also want (and have plenty of room for) a huge fridge or 'food conservation centre' with various sections which can be kept at different temperatures as well as a gadget for dispensing chilled water and ice. Don't forget the important consideration of how, through which opening and at what stage in construction the massive cooker or fridge (or indeed the large table or sofa) is going to be brought into the kitchen. It is not unheard of for such items to find a short route onto the second-hand market because they wouldn't fit through the door.

The table and chairs will by themselves create a distinct area for eating and other table-based activity, and obviously want to be next to the cooking area. Remember the issue of scale. In a large kitchen, they should be sufficiently substantial not to look silly or out of place. Comfortable seating could then be positioned in an area beyond or beside the table.

In a large kitchen with plenty of space, you can consider various options unthinkable in a smaller room. Are you a musical family? If so, why not have the piano in here? Do you live in a temperate or northern country? If so, would it give you pleasure to have an open fire or a wood burning stove in your living kitchen? Be bold, be imaginative, and aim for the kitchen of your dreams.

the futuristic kitchen

HOMEMAKERS HAVE always looked to the future with high expectations that new inventions will make life more care-free. And rightly so. Imagine life in a modern family home without a dishwasher or washing machine! What will the next step bring? Today's living kitchen already seems so full of gadgets that make so many tasks quick and easy. What next?

The futuristic kitchen is nearly with us. Already, new homes built for internet millionaires have a central computer that manages almost every aspect of the home, from room temperature and the time at which blinds or curtains are drawn to keeping track of the contents of the fridge. And it is the kitchen perhaps more than any other room that benefits from this technological leap. It is only a matter of time, we are told, before this kitchen of the future is available to almost anyone.

The kitchen computer will not only give us recipes but also tell us whether we have the ingredients in stock either because we will have scanned the contents of the fridge into its memory, or ordered our groceries through it via the internet. And by reading the barcodes on packaging it will not only know what's there but what should be eaten or disposed of today because it's close to its eat-by date. Perhaps it will even reprimand us gently if we forgetfully place raw meat above cooked on the fridge shelves.

If the kitchen is the engine room of a home, it is also the bridge. This is where practical planning for the entire household takes place, from the making of lists and discussion of arrangements when the family is gathered round the table, to the necessary paperwork relating to bills and accounts. The futuristic kitchen has a computer which stores all this information and makes it available to you at any time. It knows the sound of your voice and responds to enquiries. Via the wall-mounted terminal you can give instructions and adjust settings for all the machinery and technology in the house. It tells you what the temperature is in any room, and which doors and windows are open. In the kitchen itself, the computer will find your favourite CD and put it in the music system at the volume you require, and automatically adjust it when you answer the phone. Once you've planned the day's meals it will remind you when you should start making the soufflé and turn the oven on for you. The obvious question is: how long before the kitchen can make a soufflé on its own? Now that would be a real step into the future.

Your first expectation of a futuristic kitchen is that it will be computer controlled, but you still need to cook. Nothing beats a gas hob. Tomorrow's refinements (some available today) include sensors to detect when the flame has gone out – in which case it cuts the supply or relights – and a safety button which extinguishes all flames in an instant. Next? Why not a remote controlled computerised timer linked to the homes 'brain', so that you can ring in on the way home and get the wok heating for your stir fry?

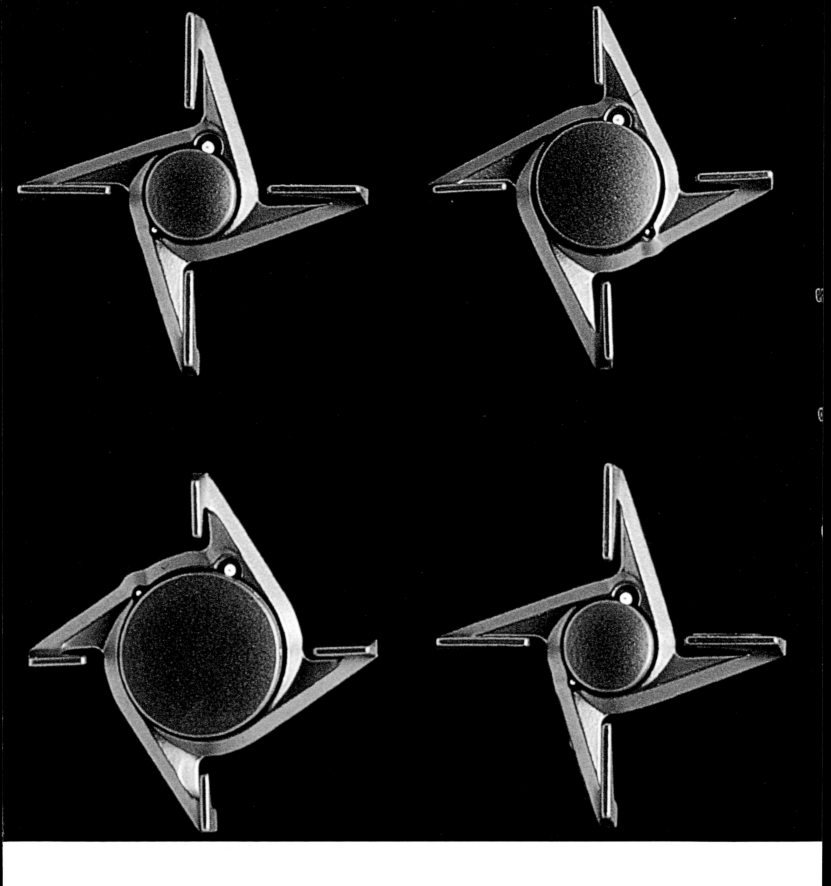

This sexy, curved, stainless-steel clad model (above) has a long list of special features, including good energy consumption and a quiet motor, 'extra cool' section for storing meat, a built-in bottle rack and the choice of crushed or cubed ice. The best of the next generation of refrigerators will think for us, with computerized displays of what's inside and what needs eating soon. This dishwasher (opposite) is designed to consume as little time, energy and water as possible, as well as automatically choosing the right programme for the load, whilst not sacrificing cleaning results.

the natural kitchen

OF ALL THE materials from which kitchens are constructed, those which age most gracefully and even when new have a particular allure, are the natural materials, wood above all others. Slate, stone and terracotta are popular too, and even cork has experienced something of a renaissance, especially now that there are products which allow us to paint or stain it. Linoleum, that classic mixture of linseed oil, cork and other natural ingredients, is back in vogue after being overlooked for a couple of generations.

Nothing could be more natural than to want a natural kitchen, but how natural is natural? It is one thing to banish plastic utensils from your kitchen and use biodegradable cleaning materials, quite another to say that you will allow no petro-chemical derivatives anywhere in the room (even those cleaning materials come in plastic bottles). This would effectively mean doing without kitchen machinery.

A middle way is to eliminate all unnecessary plastic – and you must decide what is and isn't necessary to your way of life – and choose the greenest machines available. When buying a new dishwasher, look for one that is energy efficient and uses as little water as possible. Construct a larder against a cold, outside wall so that you don't need such a big fridge for storing food. And when you do have empty plastic containers, as you inevitably will, give a thought to what happens to them next. If you simply bin them, they will probably end up on a landfill site. Instead, try to recycle as much as possible, either by reusing the containers yourself or by taking them to the nearest recycling plant.

the recycled kitchen

Recycling is an important theme in the natural kitchen, and not just the careful disposal of paper, tins and glass. An unfitted kitchen furnished with old pieces, either inherited or bought from junk (or smarter) shops, is more environmentally friendly than any newly bought fitted kitchen. Some companies making 'new' furniture, on the other hand, advertise the fact that their products are made from reclaimed wood. Likewise fabrics: if you plan to have curtains, cushions or fabric blinds, use those made from unbleached natural fibres or, if possible, fabric salvaged from older fittings. If you are laying a timber floor, or using timber elsewhere in the kitchen, try to obtain reclaimed wood for the job, or, if it's new, check that it comes from a sustainable source.

water-based paints

Developments in the paint industry in recent decades have gone in two directions. At the 'modern' end, oil-based paints have been superceded by a range of water-based versions, partly for environmental reasons. And at the other end of the scale there is the resurgence of interest in historic paints, which are perceived as being more natural and environmentally friendly. This is certainly true of the water-based paints such as limewash and distemper, both now widely available and often by mail-order. Specialist companies also offer milk paint, organic paint and other degrees of non-toxic paint and pigment, so it is no longer a battle to find natural paints to decorate your living kitchen.

CHAPTER TWO
DECORATING THE KITCHEN

BY ITS VERY NATURE, THE LIVING KITCHEN PRESENTS SOME INTERESTING DECORATING CHALLENGES. BECAUSE IT COMBINES THE FUNCTIONS OF KITCHEN, DINING ROOM AND SITTING ROOM, WE EXPECT IT TO BE WELCOMING AND COMFORTABLE AS WELL AS EFFICIENT AND HYGIENIC. THE STYLE OF THE FOOD PREPARATION AREA SHOULD MELD EFFORTLESSLY INTO THAT OF THE TABLE, CHAIRS AND OTHER FURNITURE AND FURNISHINGS. THINK OF THE ROOM AS A WHOLE, BUT WITHIN THAT WHOLE THERE CAN BE SUBTLE DIFFERENCES BETWEEN COOKING AND OTHER AREAS.

SOME STYLES from which you can choose include crisp and curvy Swedish, mellow farmhouse, industrial chic, Shaker, colourful contemporary or pale minimalist. Or choose a mixture of these to form a style that reflects your taste and the decorations in the rest of your home.

Colour is the vital element in any room's decoration, giving the room's activities a vibrant or soothing backdrop. Other significant elements include the materials and finishes of door and drawer fronts, worksurfaces, flooring … The following pages include invaluable information and tips on these and every other pertinent aspect of decorating, helping you in your choice as you design a living kitchen that looks stunning and is right for you and your household.

style

SOME POSSIBLE styles for the decoration of your living kitchen include the following:

colourful contemporary

This uses simple, bold shapes and bright, fresh colours including greens, oranges, yellows and blues (though not usually all at once – be selective), with plenty of brilliant white. Cookware and details like door and drawer knobs are stainless steel and chrome respectively. China is plain white or brightly coloured.

A subset of this category could be called 'contemporary cool' – pairing shades of jade and mist, aubergine and acqua, coffee and sun-bleached terracotta…

cool minimalist

Similar to 'colourful contemporary', with smooth, flat surfaces, stainless steel and chrome, white china and modern glass. However the colours that accompany these sleek modern materials are different: white, cream, blond wood and unbleached linen set the tone.

american diner

This uses curvy shapes, brightly coloured formica, masses of shiny chrome and chairs fatly upholstered in glossy vinyl fabric in primary colours. Expensive but fun.

shaker

Understated elegance and the beauty of finely grained woods, make this a deeply desirable and costly form of decoration. Shaker style uses simple fabrics like linen union and pure cotton, wooden bowls and artefacts, baskets and plain earthenware crocks and china.

industrial chic

This is magnificent but severe, with much stainless steel in evidence. It is suited to vast

warehouse spaces, where its scale is entirely in keeping, and urban rather than country life.

mellow farmhouse

This is the classic look, derived from the cavernous farmhouse kitchens of countries around the Mediterranean. It employs large wooden furniture, a cooking range that pulsates heat and warmth, pans and implements festooning the ceiling, and a floor of scrubbed boards or flagstones or mellow brick.

budget chic

An unpretentious style achieved through research in junk shops and local auction rooms, the decorator's main tools being pots of paint and a sewing machine with which to run up loose covers and cheerful table linen.

Examples of some of the styles you can choose from, including industrial (top right)**, colourful contemporary** (top left on this page) **and ultra-cool retro** (bottom right)**.**

crisp swedish

Gustavian grey paint on pine furniture, red and white gingham curtains and plain tableware provide the basis for this restrained, elegant look.

and colour

walls

A kitchen, especially a living kitchen, is like any other room in that the largest area of colour is likely to be that covering the walls. They offer an unmissable opportunity to influence not only the appearance but also the atmosphere of the room, through your use of colour. Bright colours like red or orange or leafy green, on even a single wall (paint the others white to help keep it fresh), will cheer you up every time you enter the room. A subtle all-over shade like sage green or milky yellow will add character to the overall scheme. Even white or cream are fine so long as they are a positive choice, not an abdication of taste.

WALLS MEAN colour in any room, including the kitchen. Before considering the colour and type of covering you want on your kitchen walls, you should have a good idea of your colour scheme for the whole room. This will depend to some extent on the style you have chosen. 'American diner' cries out for bright red, turquoise or yellow; 'Shaker' speaks gingham and natural neutrals; 'industrial chic' calls for white and bare construction materials, while 'contemporary cool' gives you scope for aubergine and sage or aqua blues and greens or bright, fresh, leaf and flower shades. A colour or range of colours can be used with white or a chalky neutral to refresh it and prevent it becoming overwhelming.

The wall at the back of a worksurface should be covered with a hard-wearing, washable finish, such as tiling or stainless steel sheeting, that will withstand heat, steam and splashing with greasy ingredients. A good-quality oil-based paint may be sufficient, and other, water-based paints promote their hard-working washability. You can also stir in a splash of anti-fungal additive to the paint before you apply it in order to enhance its manufactured qualities.

Elsewhere in the kitchen, think of this as just another room, with the added quality of being occasionally steamy. Any wallpaper you choose, for example, should be recommended by the manufacturer as being suitable for a kitchen or bathroom.

colour choices

Cool Colours

Blues and greens are traditionally thought of as cool, though certain shades of blue summon images of Greek islands and tropical summer skies and sea, enough to warm the blood of any inhabitant of temperate climes. The 'cool' connotation comes from the position of green and blue near the middle of the visible spectrum, where they retreat from and relax the eye. Fresh, contemporary shades of these colours can be used alone or in combination with each other, or with a splash of contrasting red, yellow or purple for added excitement.

Warm Colours

Reds, browns, terracotta, greys… These are restful, embracing colours that draw us into a womb-like security. They look fabulous with natural materials like wood and wicker, but their danger lies in their heat, which can make the cooking area of a kitchen feel over-hot or even oppressive. In the dining area or around comfortable seating, however, these colours are more relaxing. Pair a warmer with a cooler shade, with white or a neutral, in the hotter parts of the kitchen.

Neutrals

Paper and string, stone and chalk… these are the materials which have inspired the names of so many new paints and fabrics to emerge with the popularity of neutrals in the last decade or so. Neutrals evoke an atmosphere of restrained sophistication and also refer to the very materials from which our buildings are constructed, taking us back to basics while pampering us with luxurious textures like sheepskin, cashmere and linen. A kitchen decorated in these tones risks running the same danger as any other room – namely blandness. But neutrals can be enlivened by splashes of bright colour that lift them without overwhelming them – a picture, a throw and a collection of coloured glass on a shelf would do the trick.

Bright Colours

These are fresh and youthful, energising and fun. Use them with plenty of white or neutral shades to prevent them becoming exhausting. Alternatively, use one bright colour with paler shades of the same to restrain it somewhat – perhaps on cupboard doors and drawer fronts while the walls are stingingly vibrant.

A kitchen, especially a living kitchen, is like any other room in that the largest area of colour is likely to be that covering the walls. Your use of colour offers an unmissable opportunity to influence not only the appearance but also the atmosphere of the room. Bright colours like red or orange or leafy green, on even a single wall (paint the others white to help keep it fresh), will cheer you up every time you enter the room. A subtle all-over shade like sage green or milky-yellow will add character to the overall scheme. Even white or cream are fine so long as they are a positive choice, not an abdication of taste.

floors

Flooring is possibly the hardest element to decide upon when decorating a living kitchen because it has to fulfil so many criteria: not only must it look good but it has to last well and be immediately practical. You also have to take into account the time required to maintain it to a high standard, since this single element of the room's decoration is subject to the greatest wear. Popular choices include linoleum, timber planks and classic terracotta or quarry tiles, as well as (left, clockwise from top left) textured rubber, inlaid or printed vinyl, polished or sealed solid timber parquet and sophisticated pale stone tiles or flagstones.

THE THREE main surfaces in a room are the walls, ceiling and floor, and of the three the floor takes the most hammering. Natural materials wear best over the years – TERRACOTTA, SOLID TIMBER and LINOLEUM, for example, mellow and become even more beautiful as they develop a patina. Man-made materials like VINYL have the advantage of being cheap and cheerful, with funky designs, or photographic images of flower meadows, grass or pebbles under water. Other designs are more expensive but give an impressive imitation of floorings such as parquet and inlaid marble.

CONCRETE can be painted to alleviate its tendency to drabness; TERRAZZO has a beautiful, random pattern of marble chips; SOLID TIMBER needs careful laying and, if it does not have an underdrawing (an open space underneath), needs to be kept dry to avoid the timber buckling. Treatments and sealants for solid timber vary in glossiness and degree of water resistance, Danish oil and hard-wax oil being among the best.

Other possible kitchen floorings include:

- Slate
- Limestone
- Ceramic tiles (glazed)
- Wood laminate
- Rubber

These aluminium tiles, some smooth and some textured, offer a decisively contemporary take on the traditional floor tile on a kitchen floor.

worksurfaces

YOUR CHOICE of worksurface is a very personal one. Friends have been known to fall out over the incontrovertible superiority of one type over another – wood over colourcore, marble over stainless steel. Fashions come and go: tiles, for example, were once popular for worksurfaces, at the same time as floral stencils and Austrian blinds.

Today, stainless steel and solid timber are probably at the front of the field, with stainless steel a fraction ahead. The latter can be affordable: buy a sheet from a steel stock holder, give it to a metal cutter to shape, together with a template made from hardboard, and finish it yourself with a file. Be extremely careful, wearing protective gloves, goggles and clothing. Glue the stainless steel to a worktop made of marine plywood, in situ, and paint the edge to match other elements in the room's decoration.

Everyone has their favourite material for worksurfaces; none of them is perfect. The factors to assess and to question the salespeople about include:

- **Colour**
- **Texture**
- **Cost**
- **Ease of installation**
- **Maintenance**
- **Hardwearing quality**
- **Modernity**
- **Cleaning routine**
- **Classic quality**

The ideal kitchen has different worksurfaces in different areas: a heatproof material next to the cooker for placing hot pans on, a marble slab for rolling pastry, a wooden area for preparing vegetables or slicing bread. But a square of the relevant material laid on top of the worksurface serves just as well, and offers a solution available to most of us, however small our budget.

There is a huge variety of worksurfaces to choose from – almost a baffling choice. Balance your dreams with your first-hand knowledge of materials and friends' and professionals' recommendations. Possible alternatives, some more contemporary or predictable than others include (clockwise from top left) clear glass; contemporary cutting-edge; stainless steel, which becomes more beautiful with age like all the classic worksurface materials; oiled or polished wood, its patina building with age and its rich natural surface giving pleasure to generations of cooks; polished slate, one of many traditional materials given a new life by contemporary technology.

knobs and handles

IT IS wonderful the impact that such small items as knobs and handles can have on the appearance of a kitchen. Replace the fancy antiqued brass knobs which were just the thing in the 1970s with plain, shiny chrome knobs and see your cupboard doors look younger, fresher and suddenly contemporary.

Knobs and handles need to be practical – not too small or too large, and easy to grip, even if your hand is greasy or floury. Run your hand over and around a wide selection in the shop to convince yourself that you like the feel before making a final decision, and be prepared to take them back if your choice proves not to look quite right in situ. If in doubt, go for something simple.

You can also customize knobs by buying plain, unvarnished wooden ones and painting them yourself, to match other colours in the room. You could even paint on or stencil a personal motif, or get your children to paint patterns on them for some original naïve artistic touches around the kitchen.

As a general rule, knobs and handles should contrast with the material of the cupboard door or drawer front. If your drawers are painted, by all means have shiny or matt silver-coloured knobs, but if your kitchen units have a metallic finish, black metal knobs, or coloured glass, would be better. Knobs and handles are an important design detail, after all.

Knobs and handles for the drawers and cupboards in your kitchen are available in a vast choice of materials and designs. The plainest, white wooden handles can be the best choice for a simple, spare design (right). **At the other end of the spectrum, these funky, space-age knobs** (left) **have marbles of coloured glass set into them for an insant, up-to-the-minute look.**

Wrought iron is one of the oldest materials from which handles are made, yet even this has been reinterpreted to live happily in the contemporary kitchen (below, right), as with these sensuous curves. Traditional wrought iron styles (below, left) can be sleek, discreet and practical. Chrome and stainless steel knobs and handles (right) vary widely too. These are satin smooth and cleverly designed to make a marked but understated contribution to the finish of any interior.

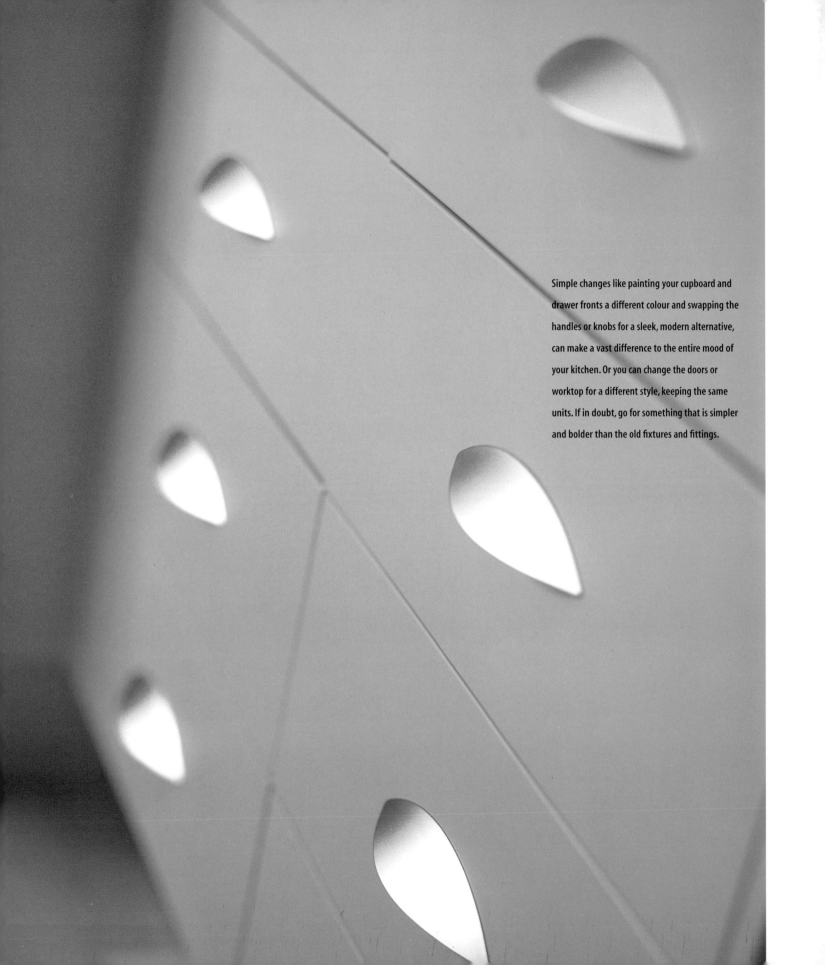

Simple changes like painting your cupboard and drawer fronts a different colour and swapping the handles or knobs for a sleek, modern alternative, can make a vast difference to the entire mood of your kitchen. Or you can change the doors or worktop for a different style, keeping the same units. If in doubt, go for something that is simpler and bolder than the old fixtures and fittings.

updating an existing kitchen

THERE ARE several reasons why you might want to update an existing kitchen. You might have moved to a new home and not have the budget for a new kitchen, or you might be renting a property, or you might feel that your kitchen, much loved though it has been over the years, is simply looking dated and in need of a face-lift.

The first thing to do if you want to update a kitchen is to give it a massive and thorough clean. Then consider all the items that you can do without or put away – sorting and organising your possessions can simplify and modernise a kitchen to an astonishing degree. Aim to kill the clutter, for good, and this includes any fancy bits or frills. Fussiness is the enemy of freshness.

Next, look at each of the following items, in isolation and in relation to each other, and decide what has to go and what can be adapted to a fresher, more contemporary look. Cupboard doors and drawer fronts, for example, can be replaced or painted, or their centre panels replaced with glass or wire mesh, without the entire unit being sacrificed. Even 'white goods' can be painted. Give them a good clean and sanding first, so that the paint can get a grip, and spray with car paint or brush on a hardwearing paint in a colour that ties in with your scheme for the room. Replacing wall cupboards with open shelves might open up the room and make it feel bigger. Changing the colour scheme can update and uplift a room – paint is a wonderfully cheap and easy decorating material.

Make a schedule of the work you would like tradesmen such as a plumber or electrician to do in the room to update it, with each item listed separately. Ask more than one tradesman for a price for the work and choose not only whom you want to do the job but also exactly how many of the items on your list you can actually afford.

A checklist of items to update:

- **Cupboard doors**
- **Drawer fronts**
- **Knobs and handles**
- **Worksurface**
- **White goods like fridge and dishwasher**
- **Flooring**
- **Wall cupboards**
- **Shelving**
- **Lighting and sockets**
- **Furniture**

a budget kitchen from scratch

IN THIS situation you are faced with an empty room and a small budget with which to create a welcoming, practical living kitchen. Where do you start? Assuming that all aspects of the room, including windows and doors, are structurally sound, where do you begin? The three most vital elements are the cooker, the sink and the table. A reconditioned, second-hand cooker (and indeed fridge) from a reputable outlet can give you several years' service. A sink can be inexpensively installed on simple timber legs, if the budget does not run to a supporting unit. Build a shelf under this and store items neatly in a row of matching boxes or baskets, or hang a curtain to hide buckets and cleaning materials.

The wiring and plumbing of such items as sink and cooker, and the wiring of the room for lighting and sockets, is obviously not something that you can scrimp on, in the interest of safety. But if you know far enough ahead that you are going to undertake a project of this scale you could acquire some training at evening classes in advance. Alternatively, many areas offer a labour barter scheme, whereby a person does work for you in which they are skilled in return for your services in another area (anything from accountancy to bread-making), not necessarily

supplied to the same person.

Inexpensive tables can be found in a variety of outlets, from the high street and chain stores to junk shops and sale rooms. Don't worry if the surface is 'ruined': you can almost certainly revive this with sanding and paint or varnish. The important thing is structure – is the table sturdy on its legs? Chairs ditto, and don't worry if they don't match each other – a lick of paint will unify them wonderfully. Don't forget that a table can have a new top attached, and a chair a new seat. Sturdiness is the basic requirement. (See also page 82.)

Paint is the great ally of the budget decorator. It is relatively extremely cheap, widely available and offered in a dazzling range of colours to cheer your eyes and your heart, especially if you are seriously impoverished. Use it not only on walls, ceiling, woodwork and furniture but also on the floor. Boards and concrete floors can be painted with the appropriate products (increasingly available in wonderful colours), either plain or with an interesting pattern. A floor in poor condition can be covered with timber sheeting of various types, varying in finish and cost, and then sealed or painted. Or you can lay cork tiles, dreary in

themselves but receptive to all sorts of paints and hard-wax oil, so long as they are initially unsealed. Create a pattern with tiles painted (separately) in two or more colours.

Worksurfaces can be supplied by old furniture, raised to the right height and decorated according to your scheme for the whole room, or by supporting a length of inexpensive counter top bought from a DIY outlet on a simple timber frame. Look out for old enamel and marble slabs which will provide you with resilient and handsome food preparation areas. Storage beneath can be provided by various racks and trolleys, with or without casters, and stacking boxes. If your budget runs to inexpensive fitted units with worktop and cupboards, even along one wall, this will repay you with the maximum amount of storage possible in the space, and a tidy look. Shop around and ask about sales and ex-showroom kitchens.

A kitchen doesn't have to be a temple to all that is sleek and modern. In this living kitchen, the old-fashioned reconditioned fridge stands in the corner and an old radio perches on a shelf. But the toaster and espresso machine (on top of the fridge) are state of the art, though their curving forms are retro in inspiration. Other furniture in the room is antique wooden, but old cupboards and tables found in places like auctions, thrift stores and junk shops would do the job just as well. An unfitted kitchen with freestanding furniture looks more like a real 'room' than one with fitted units, and the fact that you can see all the way to the walls, rather than your view being halted by fitted furniture, makes it seems larger too. Extra storage space found for a few objects on a single shelf high up on the wall has the effect of leading your eye up to the full height of the ceiling.

IT IS in the nature of the living kitchen that it should be a flexible space, as welcoming to children's cooking, homework or art creations as to visiting friends. This flexibility is demanding, requiring improvisation, practical changes and different atmospheres often at very short notice. Here are some useful ideas for quick changes in your kitchen.

homework

Given free rein, homework can quickly take over the kitchen, especially if you have more than one child. Books, papers, pens, maps, reference works - the clutter spells industry, but it can get out of hand. And what to do if you have unexpected visitors, or your child simply runs out of time to finish her project today? If homework is a regular

quick changes

occurrence in the kitchen, you need to assign an area of storage to it, however small. This could be a basket or box on a shelf within the child's reach, in which they know they will always find pencil, sharpener, dictionary and foolscap. Half a cupboard or just a box in a cupboard can be devoted to art stuffs, and part of a shelf made over to books. Be prepared to police these spaces - you don't want the kitchen to become a dumping ground for anything and everything.

home office

Household management may seem an antiquated idea, but it is as necessary today as it was in the heyday of grand country houses - as anyone who has ever run a home knows - and the kitchen table can be the perfect desk. For storing papers, you may prefer to keep a filing cabinet in another room, or you could invest in one that looks like an ordinary piece of furniture in a traditional or contemporary style. If you are having a kitchen specially designed for you, remember to ask for drawers for hanging files and paperwork.

Current documents to which you will want to refer can be kept in a ring binder on the shelf with your cookbooks, with items such as loose receipts and stationery organised in labelled boxes or folders. If your main desk is elsewhere,

and you simply want a place for gathering loose papers as they come in, use a discreet in-tray or a garden trug.

dinner-party atmosphere

Of course, you can transform your kitchen table simply by flicking a clean cloth onto it, but there are two other vital elements that can instantly alter the atmosphere of your kitchen from family room to dinner-party location: lighting and scent. Light a candle with an exotic or subtle scent such as jasmine, sweet orange or bergamot a few minutes before your guests are due to arrive to allow it to permeate the room; then adjust the lights. Lighting technology and design has advanced hugely and we expect much more variety and sophistication from kitchen lighting than the fluorescent strip which lit so many kitchens twenty years ago. Unless the lighting in your kitchen has been updated quite recently, you may feel frustrated that you cannot vary the areas and quality of light. Don't forget, however, that you can bring lamps into the kitchen. A desk lamp with an adjustable head can be used to direct light onto a work surface or serving area, allowing you to turn off the main lights, while the table can be lit by candles or hurricane lamps. A standard lamp or floor-standing uplighter will give ambient light without dazzling.

the television

If you have plenty of room in your kitchen for people to sit around comfortably, or if you are an addict of soap operas or the news, you may want to have a television in the kitchen. Try to avoid putting it on or near the floor as it will tend to dominate the space around it. A very small television can be discreet and sit happily on a shelf or in a cupboard, to be revealed only when you want to watch. A medium-sized television will fit on a shelf or be supported by a wall bracket. A really large television is heavy and needs serious support, either from a sturdy piece of freestanding furniture or a custom-made built-in structure.

The television in a large living kitchen with space for a sofa and chairs may be the home's main focus for tele-viewing. In this case, for rapid transformation (or at least disguise), group all the audio and visual kit in one place and have a sliding or folding screen which can easily be drawn to hide it at a moment's notice.

trouble shooting

EVEN THE most wonderful living kitchen may have some little fault, some element, however small, that you would do differently if you were starting again. Sometimes these things emerge only when you start using the kitchen after long planning and construction; often they are things you have to live with because you inherited them from your home's previous owner. Either way, don't despair! Here are some tips for tackling the most likely problems.

sink or other spot too dark

You can attack this problem from several angles. The best thing to do is of course to add light. Today, light fittings have become so small and clever, and the light from even a tiny halogen bulb is so bright and clean, that it is the easiest thing simply to install a small spotlight that clips onto a shelf and has an adjustable head so that you can direct the light onto the sink or other trouble spot. Have two, even, one each side. If the clip-on light is to be semi-permanent, fix the flex against the wall and paint it the same colour. It might also be possible to install baffle lighting tucked under wall-mounted cupboards, or fix a small directional spotlight there.

Another approach is to hang a mirror where it will reflect light into the dark corner. Alternatively, face the back of the dark area with metallic-finish tiles, now available in various tones and degrees of shine, with a sheet of stainless steel, or with mirror tiles, though in a working area you will have to put some effort into keeping these clean.

not enough worksurface

However much worksurface you have, there never seems to be enough. In a small kitchen, however, this can be a real problem. Start by taking everything off the existing worksurfaces and sorting through your things. Find other places to keep as many items as possible, discard things you don't really use, and raise essential items such as the microwave or kettle up off the worksurface onto a shelf or bracket. If you can lift such pieces of equipment even six inches this will suddenly make the space beneath available. A cluster of olive oil and vinegar bottles can be lifted onto a shallow shelf near the cooker.

Once you've done this, consider adding a portable work surface. A trolley with lockable castors and a solid timber top will give you more work space, plus you'll be able to move it out of the way when it's not in use. Yet another alternative is to have a fold-down or fold-up counter that lies flat against the wall when not in use but can be swung into action when you are preparing a meal or need to serve up.

Not enough worksurface? Hob too dark? Both problems can be solved without upheaval or recourse to major financial expenditure. Lighten up the hob or sink or other dingy corners with a combination of discreet spotlights and some reflective decorating materials like these metallic sheen tiles (above), placed strategically to make the most of what light there is. When positioning spotlights remember to take into account the direction in which it will cast shadows (your own as you lean over a pan, for example). For added workspace, invest in a freestanding table like this (left, above) which is not only the same height as worksurface (a table for sitting and eating at is usually lower) but also incorporates two types of storage. Small items like hand-held gadgets, dish cloths and drying up clothes, napkins and napkin rings, can be kept together in the drawers while the rack below is sturdy enough to accommodate a collection of cookware. Alternatively, you might choose a trolley (left, below) with castors which has a solid timber top and storage below. This can be moved from place to place in the room, depending on the job to be done.

A tall, neat, freestanding cupboard like this (below) could be fitted into a narrow space to provide extra storage space, both inside and on top. This freestanding drying rack (opposite, top) is a work of art in itself, amusing to look at and, when not in use, light enough to hang up on a hook out of the way. A folding drying rack is useful where space is short as you can close it and slide it away out of sight between uses. Implements like spoons and ladles (opposite, below left) can be hung from a rail if there are not enough drawers, while open shelves (opposite, below right) offer storage whilst at the same time seeming open and airy.

no built-in rubbish bin

Freestanding bins aren't so bad – some people actually prefer them. The design of kitchen bins has come a long way, and though there's still room for improvement, you are almost certain to find a model that looks good in your kitchen, whatever its style. Hiding the bin bag may be more of a problem. Take a plastic sack with you to experiment with different models in the shop. Test the efficiency of the foot pedal, the weight of the cover that you'll have to lift in order to empty it, or the ease with which it moves if it's on castors. Think positive. The great charm of a freestanding bin is that you can take it to the debris, rather than always having to cart your rubbish around the room.

too few drawers

What can the previous owners have been thinking of? Where did they keep their gadgets, wooden spoons, table napkins, mats, corkscrew? Their habits may be a mystery, but the lack of drawer space is a plain inconvenience. There are three routes open to you: either store fewer items in drawers, get some freestanding drawers, or convert existing storage space into 'drawers'. This last option is less radical than it sounds. Open shelves, for example, can offer storage for lots of small items with the help of the many

different storage boxes now available. If you plan to store fewer things in the drawers, first decide what these should be. The obvious candidates are the many small items, and the things you use the most. Others such as wooden spoons or metal cooking implements can be stood upright in jars on a windowsill or counter top, or hung from a rail or rack. Cutlery can be organised in a wicker or wooden tray divided into sections for the purpose. Table napkins can be stored in a basket in which they can easily be carried to the table. Finally, some trolleys also have drawers and racks beneath their worksurface, so you'll be able to solve the problem of work space and drawer space in one go.

not enough storage

The question to ask yourself is: 'storage for what?' This might be a good moment to have a huge clear-out. Get to the back of the cupboards and the bottom of the drawers and take a good look at your possessions. Consider which items get regular use and keep them handy. If you have large pieces of cookware that you don't often use – a fish kettle or enormous casserole, for instance – is there somewhere else you could keep them? Perhaps the cellar or the garage? Find yourself a back-up storage space in another room or in an inaccessible corner of the kitchen, somewhere to put items which you want to keep but which don't have to be always to hand. At the same time, look for wasted storage space in the kitchen itself. You could fix a shelf to the top part of the wall, for example, and have either a row of objects on display or a row of identical containers such as boxes for gathering together smaller items.

Even having taken these measures, you may still find you haven't enough space, especially if your life and family demands mean that you have to store plenty of food between fortnightly visits to the supermarket. In this case, examine the insides of your cupboards. Is there wasted space between the top of a row of packets or glasses and the bottom of the next shelf up? If so, you can use this space by inserting a wire rack on the shelf below or hanging a shelf-basket from the shelf above. Empty space between open shelves can be used by screwing cup hooks from which to hang mugs, cups and jugs. But do consider carefully which of these to have on display to prevent the place looking a jumble. As elsewhere in the house, the secret to tallying your possessions with the amount of storage space is to edit, edit, edit.

CHAPTER THREE

TABLES AND CHAIRS

THE TABLE, WITH ITS CHAIRS AROUND IT, IS AT THE HEART OF THE LIVING KITCHEN. THE IDEAL TABLE FULFILS A WIDE RANGE OF FUNCTIONS. AT ONE MOMENT IT PROVIDES EXTRA WORKING SPACE FOR FOOD PREPARATION, AT ANOTHER IT IS A WORKBENCH FOR THE FAMILY'S ART AND CRAFT ACTIVITIES OR A QUIET PLACE FOR HOMEWORK, STUDY OR HOUSEHOLD PAPERWORK. AT ONE MOMENT IT IS THE PLACE TO LINGER WITH A LOVED ONE OVER AN INTIMATE MEAL OF DELICACIES, AT ANOTHER IT IS HOST TO A BOISTEROUS SUNDAY LUNCH OR BIRTHDAY DINNER PARTY.

THE KITCHEN table needs to be hardworking, handsome and versatile. It is also the largest single piece of furniture, its appearance dominating the available space, whether your kitchen is large or small. Tables come in a huge variety of styles, materials, finishes and mechanisms – wood, metal, glass, modern, antique, folding, swivel-topped, extending… This chapter guides you through the possibilities.

Chairs are important too, and are made in an equally wide range of materials, though not always the same ones. They can be regal in a huge kitchen, wiry and strong in a tiny one. They can be elegant or simply practical, stacking or folding to create space. Chairs can also be colourful – all the same colour or many different colours. Old or tired-looking chairs can be transformed with paint and other finishes so that they become part of the room's overall decorative scheme – this chapter tells you how.

Tables come in almost as many shapes, sizes and designs as there are types of people to sit round them. When considering a table, draw a chair up to it so that you can experience sitting at it, to check that it is a comfortable height and that you like it. Be realistic – if you choose a glass-topped table are you going to be exhausted worrying that your children will break it (unlikely, since glass tops are made of dense, tough-ened material)? Relax and choose a style and size that matches your needs. It might be topped with aluminium sheeting (above), or it might be timber in a classic timeless design or in a contemporary style (opposite above and below). Think of your table as an investment.

the table

IF THERE is one element in a living kitchen that could be said to be the focus of the room, it is the table. It is at the table that most social activity takes place. Here you feed the brood, gather with family and friends to eat and drink, or sit for a quiet meal with your loved one; here you perch to do paperwork and make all those lists required by the demands of household management and the organisation of special occasions; here the children (or indeed adults) sit to do homework or craftwork; here is the place for a wide range of routine household activities, from preparing vegetables to polishing shoes to writing the Christmas cards. In fact, so much happens at the kitchen table that it is a marvel that the type of so-called 'kitchen table' novelist or dressmaker famous in the 1970s and '80s ever got anything done.

The table obviously has to fulfil a variety of requirements. It must be good-looking, as indeed should every element of the kitchen, but it is often unique in being the only independent piece of furniture, standing alone and therefore seen in its entirety (even if you have an unfitted kitchen, most other pieces are against a wall). It should be hard-

wearing. And in a living kitchen it needs to be versatile.

Versatility in a table takes several forms. It should be able to withstand the wear and tear of hard daily use without looking disgusting, and yet be readily transformed into the serene setting for a dinner party. It should be of a practical size, in keeping with both your needs and the space for it in the kitchen, yet able, ideally, to become larger or smaller as circumstance demands. The table might even offer storage space, if it has drawers.

choosing a table

The following is a checklist of considerations when you are choosing a table:

- **Where exactly is the table going to stand?**
- **Does it need to be moved around?**
- **Does it need to be folded/slid away when not in use?**

- How much space is needed around it for people to sit and move, and move when others are sitting?
- How many people will usually be sitting down at it and do they have any special requirements (eg high chair, wheelchair)?
- What is the best shape of table for your space: square, rectangular, round, oval, semi-circular, elliptical, a shape specially made to fit?
- Do you entertain often and if so, how many people do you like to seat?
- Besides being a table for eating at, what other main activities does it host?

space and storage

These are vital considerations when you are planning your type of table, the more so the smaller your kitchen. Here are some ideas for tables which change size:

- Tables which fold up or down against the wall. If up, you need a bar catch or other method to secure it from falling accidentally
- Gateleg table, where the two ends fold down leaving a narrow section of top covering the legs folded beneath. One half can be lowered for everyday use but you can't sit at the side where the other half is folded down (fine if it's against a wall, for example)
- Table which folds away completely into a kitchen unit.

Ingenious but remember that it deprives you of a cupboard for storage

- Table which slides out from under the counter top. Note that you will need tall chairs or stools in order to sit level with it
- Extra leaves which can be inserted to make a table larger. These are either completely removable, as with an antique dining table, in which case you need somewhere to store the extra leaves, or they fold away under the middle of the everyday table top (the modern option)
- False top. Cut a piece of chipboard or other timber to a larger size than your table (and perhaps even a different shape too – round instead of square, for example) and place it over the top for special occasions. Paint the false top decoratively or cover it with a cloth. This, too, needs to be stored when not in use
- Garden furniture. Some designs, including lightweight, folding furniture made from slatted wood or resin and held together with metal strips, look as good indoors as out, and if light enough can be stored hung on the wall. A slatted table needs a cloth to prevent cutlery from falling through the gaps at meal times.

A table like this makes a strong
visual statement. It is substantial
and uncompromisingly
contemporary, using as it does two
popular materials, pale wood and
stainless steel. The curving legs
give it elegance.

table
styles and materials

WHEN YOU are thinking about the different styles of table and the materials of which they are made, a new and vital consideration comes to the fore: what the table looks like. Its appearance clearly wants to be in keeping with the rest of the kitchen; indeed, it may be the starting point for a decorative scheme.

wooden tables

The most traditional form of kitchen table, the one which evokes the archetypal Mediterranean farmhouse setting, is wooden. Today, exactly such tables can be obtained from shops selling goods imported from France and Italy (or obtained locally, if you live in or visit either of these countries). There are plenty of wooden alternatives, however, from battered old antique examples to sleek, contemporary designs which would not look out of place in a minimalist setting. Wood is never out of fashion.

You may have or want a fine wooden table, antique or modern, to enjoy on special occasions, but be nervous about damaging it during everyday use. Some varnishes are supposedly heatproof but French polish (the usual finish on antique furniture) certainly is not (and neither is it waterproof). However, it is possible to combine a fine finish with practicality, by protecting the table for daily use with a

specially made-to-fit heatproof and waterproof cover. Rather like a large mat, such a cover can be bought from specialist suppliers and is effective but not usually attractive in appearance. You will probably want to put a table cloth over the cover. For every day this could be a plastic-coated cloth – perhaps brightly coloured or patterned to contrast further with the sober appearance of the fine table beneath – which is easy to swab down. Other fabric cloths can be laid over the top or alternated with it for smarter occasions or simply for fun.

The scrubbed pine table is a kitchen classic which survives from the early decades of the nineteenth century and before. Examples from a hundred years ago are still quite readily found. Typically, this type of table has a wooden top constructed from panels of pine with extra leaves slid in underneath for expansion to nearly double its size. The top is not sealed in any way by wax or varnish. This allows you to rub it clean with a cloth and hot soapy water or scouring powder. Unpolished wood is naturally regenerative to an astonishing degree – indeed scientists are said to have discovered that it has naturally occurring antibacterial qualities when rubbed or scrubbed.

Like the table on the previous page, this handsome example (opposite) **has a polished wooden top and metal base, but here the metal is in the form of curled, wrought iron legs which look playful and pretty.**

classic tables

There are many other classic kitchen tables, from the chrome American diner style (with matching fatly upholstered chairs) to the 1950s and '60s turquoise-topped melamine laminate example. Shaker tables are exceptionally elegant and none the less practical for that.

future classics

Which tables will become the classics of the future? Current design is characterized by variety, in keeping with the multifarious decorating styles which feed our culture of choice, and by ingenuity. Tables not only fold (as they have done for centuries) but can fold away completely. A table can have a reversible top with, perhaps, practical laminate on one side and more formal polished wood on the other. Even if you want a traditional wooden 'farmhouse' table, this comes in many different styles and can even be made up to your order after you have chosen a top and a base from the manufacturer's range. Another option is, of course, to have a table especially designed and created for you by a furniture maker, or to design your own and have a joiner construct it.

Here is a list of styles, materials, combinations of material, and types to help you define your own ideas:

- **Suitable woods include: pine, oak, beech, ash, cherry, maple**
- **Wooden top made from pitched pine boards or scaffolding planks**
- Laminate top in a bright or pastel colour
- Tiled table top, or mosaic top made from broken tiles
- Polished slate top, or marble, or limestone
- Glass top, toughened and thick enough to be rigid (generally around 1cm), possibly acid etched for a frosted, misty finish
- Trestles made of wood or metal
- Base made from wood or metals such as stainless steel, scaffolding poles, wrought iron, or finished with powder coating, chrome or paint.

revamping an old table

Check first that the table really is worth the effort – that it stands firmly four-square without being warped or rickety or worm-eaten. Then clean it by scrubbing with a hot solution of soda crystals (wear gloves to protect your hands and use an effective brush) and/or stripping old varnish or paint.

If you decide to paint the table, create a pattern on it which is relevant to you and your kitchen: your initials or the date, or a motif taken from your china or other decorations in the room.

Alternatively, sand and seal the bare wood with varnish, perhaps giving it a coat of colourwash first, or fix a sheet of plain or coloured glass or plastic to the top, perhaps with metal corners. Old laminate can be removed and replaced, so long as the timber underneath has not warped or buckled.

There are countless different styles of traditional chair suitable for the living kitchen. These (opposite) are both substantial and geometrical. Other styles are more curvaceous, some with turned elements. The chair at far right is a rugged pine farmhouse type; the nearer chair has an elegance and line reminiscent of the great Art Nouveau designer Charles Rennie Mackintosh (1868-1928).

chairs: traditonal

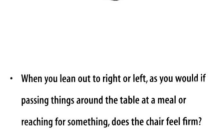

CHAIRS, MEANWHILE, have a set of requirements of their own. In practical terms, they must be extraordinarily hardwearing. Probably no other furniture in the home gets shoved about as much as kitchen chairs. They are sat upon, obviously, but this alone can be too much for a lightweight, flimsy chair or one that is simply old, especially if you have a habit of tipping your chair back onto its rear legs.

At some point in their lives kitchen chairs almost inevitably double as ships and castles for children and footstools for adults reaching inaccessible shelves and cupboards. They are pushed in and out from the table with hands and feet, and stood hard up against each other when there are extra visitors to be fitted around the table at a meal.

A chair that is in daily use must also be comfortable. It really is advisable to sit in a chair before buying it, even if you eventually make the purchase by mail order. Sit down firmly, well back on the seat, at a table of the same height as yours, and wriggle about a bit.

Consider the following points carefully, without hurrying.

- First impression: is the chair remotely comfortable?
- Is the seat deep enough from back to front to support your legs properly, and is it wide enough?
- Does the back support yours properly, especially when you lean back?
- If it has arms, are they at the right height?
- Can you tuck your feet under easily, or do the legs get in the way?

- When you lean out to right or left, as you would if passing things around the table at a meal or reaching for something, does the chair feel firm?
- Is the seat the right height off the floor for your comfort, and for you to fit happily under the table?
- When you push the chair backwards on the floor whilst sitting on it (as people do when getting up from table) does it fall over backwards?
- Do you feel good sitting in this chair?

chairs: modern

Contemporary chairs and stools take so many forms – whole shops are devoted to them – that you are almost bound to find one you like and which looks good in your kitchen. Some designs are colourful (like these upholstered chairs, bottom right), others almost austere in their simplicity (the bent plywood example, top right). Other designs are humourous or practical, such as stools which stack or screw up or down to suit your height. The stools top left are built like drums, the one below has an organically-shaped wooden seat intended to be blissfully comfortable because it is sympathetic to the shape of the human form.

size and scale

Consider also how practical or otherwise the chair is in terms of space. A chair can fulfil all your other requirements but simply not fit around your table in the numbers you want. The legs of some chairs splay out slightly (some models of bent plywood chair with chrome legs, in the style of the delicious, classic 1950s Arne Jacobsen butterfly design, are notorious for this), take up more room around the table than you might think, and can also become entangled with each other. They can trip up either you or (more likely) frail members of the family.

Conversely, if you have an enormous living kitchen, chairs that are too small may look lost and insignificant. In this situation you want a design of chair that is not only substantial, perhaps with a luxuriously bulky upholstered seat, but that includes extra tall or large chairs for the ends of the table. These might have arms while the others do not, in the style of traditional 'carver' chairs in antique suites of furniture, or you may have room for every chair to offer the comfort of arms.

the versatile chair

As with the table, your choice of kitchen chair needs to earn its keep through versatility, both when in use and when not in use. Here are some possible considerations which you can match to your habits and needs:

- Does this design of chair stack?
- Does it fold?
- Will it hang on the wall or fit into my cupboard?
- Is it lightweight and easily carried from one room to another depending on where it is needed?
- Does the design of the back allow me to hang my jacket or scarf on it without it slipping off?
- Does this chair require special maintenance, such as polishing with wax?
- Can I easily sling a cotton cover over it to transform its appearance for special occasions or according to the season?
- Can it be used in the garden, on the terrace, as well as in the house?

styles and materials

Like tables, chairs come in a dazzling variety of styles, designs and materials, but not always the same ones as tables. Chairs are not made of glass, for example, but clear plastic ones are similar in appearance. Chairs come in woven paper (Lloyd Loom), moulded plastic and Perspex as well as more predictable materials like wood and metal. Put simply, your choice is to have chairs which match or complement the material from which your table is made, or which contrast with it. You also have the choice of having chairs which match each other, or which don't.

A collection of single chairs can be unified by being painted the same colour. Some styles of chair, such as those inspired by Arne Jacobsen designs (and the originals too), come in one design but several colours, from which you could make a set from one, two, three or more colours, or have each chair a different colour. Such a carnival effect needs to be married with a plain table if the effect is not to become exhaustingly busy.

stools and benches

When it comes to versatility, one item of seating above all others has earned itself a devoted and enthusiastic fan following: the stool. Stools have a long pedigree – they are probably the oldest style of manmade seating. Stools tuck away neatly when not in use. Some stack. They double as small tables. They tend to take up less space than chairs and, of course, they cannot be seen below the level of the table which gives the kitchen a clear, uncluttered appearance.

A bench is an extension of this principal and an even more practical one if there is any number of people to be seated in a confined space. Place a long bench against the wall and set the table against this. Some benches have a back to them, which makes them more leisurely and negates the argument that a bench or stool gives you no support as you sit.

Furniture designs of the 1950s by Arne Jacobsen are hugely popular again and have spawned a number of adoring imitations which are available in a mouthwatering choice of colours.

chairs:functional

Anodised metal chairs (top left) come in various colours, and when folded away are so slim that they make storage easy. Stacking chairs (top right) are practical, the form of these inspired by Arne Jacobsen's 1950s classic; more stacking chairs (bottom right), these almost severely elegant and contemporary; and outdoors-indoors (bottom left): the classic, slatted, folding garden chair, reinterpreted for the 21st century in resin and steel, and as comfortable indoors as out.

CHAPTER FOUR

FINISHING TOUCHES

YOUR KITCHEN IS PLANNED, CONSTRUCTED AND DECORATED. NOW IT NEEDS THOSE FINISHING TOUCHES TO GIVE IT THAT INDEFINABLE QUALITY – STYLE. GLORIOUS AS SHOW KITCHENS AND THE BROCHURES ARE (AND OTHER PEOPLE'S BRAND NEW KITCHENS) WHAT YOU WANT IS A ROOM THAT REFLECTS YOU, YOUR TASTES AND LIFESTYLE. IT IS THE LITTLE THINGS AS MUCH AS THE OVERALL DESIGN THAT WILL MAKE THIS LIVING KITCHEN UNIQUELY YOURS.

CHINA AND glass, for example, can be used decoratively if there is the wall-space to display it. So can antique kitchen utensils. Pictures and other artworks add essential decoration to otherwise bare walls. Rugs not only give warmth and comfort and a change of texture underfoot but can also be used to divide space, indicating where one activity ends and another begins. Candles, especially deliciously scented ones, help create extra atmosphere.

Fabric has its place in the living kitchen – in covers and cushions for chairs and seating, and on the table as tablecloths and napkins (different ones for different occasions and moods). Window treatment is another important detail – the kitchen should be as warm and cosy in winter as it is light and airy in summer.

glass

ONE OF the most appealing corners of an interiors shop is the glassware department where shelf upon shelf of regimented rows of sparkling glasses, jugs and bowls, some in jewel-like colours, are displayed. Of course, in a shop the glasses are almost untouched, with a polished virginity that seems to set them apart. They are also cleverly lit to enhance their glittering appearance.

Even at home, serried ranks of brilliantly clean glasses on an open shelf have something of the same magic but those which are mottled with dishwasher soap, finger marks or dust, do not. Store glasses well away from the cooking area, to prevent them picking up grease from the air, and rinse and dry them after dishwashing if necessary. If there are spotlights on the kitchen ceiling, you can point one at the glassware to highlight its sparkle.

Today there is a huge range of everyday glassware available in traditional and contemporary forms and colours, and many different styles of crystal, too, if you are prepared to invest in it. Consider what you like to drink and have glasses appropriate to your own tastes and those of all the other household members.

It's useful, for example, to have tumblers of different sizes – smaller ones for children or an aperitif, larger for water for adults. Small wine glasses can seem rather mean, but are useful for sherry, fortified wines or sweet dessert wine. Enormous wine goblets look handsome but have at least one disadvantage; it is tempting to fill them in proportion with the size of the glass, which means that you or your guests may drink more than you realize. Such generous glasses are perfect for refreshing summer cups, on the other hand, having plenty of room for bits of fruit and ice. Large goblets are also more easily knocked over and broken, as are unusually tall glasses. Champagne, however, should always be drunk from tall, narrow flutes to conserve the fizz.

Contemporary coloured glass comes in a wide variety of designs that will lend a touch of glamour to all styles of living kitchen, including the neo-baroque hand made (main picture) and the super-sleek and witty post-modernist (far left). **Crystal** (near left), **too, is** available in both traditional and modern styles, as these classic goblets and knubbly champagne flutes illustrate.

A SERVICE of fine china quickly becomes an heirloom, passing from one generation to another, each owner gaining pleasure from the thought that this practical and beautiful possession has been enjoyed by his or her forebears. The disadvantage of inheriting a dinner (or other) service is that if you don't like it there's nothing you can do except hide it away, until your taste, or fashion, changes.

Everyday china is another matter. Not only do you choose it but you also enjoy it day after day. Moreover, it makes a significant contribution to the style of a kitchen. Are you a colourful, handpainted Italian sort of person, or a restrained flat white minimalist? Does your kitchen call for a mix of designs and patterns but all in blue and white, or for perfectly matching, 1950s-inspired multicoloured china with white spots? Have a

china

good look around the shops and in the catalogues and decide what will suit your kitchen and your aspirations, as well as your purse.

When choosing, remember that everyday china will see heavy use by all members of the household and is likely to get broken. Bone china breaks slightly less easily than earthenware but is more expensive to replace. China in a standard design from a local or high street store, or reputable mail-order company, should be easy to replace – an important consideration. Alternatively, buy lots more of it than necessary and keep a reserve of the most-used items (probably dinner plates, side plates and mugs) to replace breakages.

One of the most useful pieces is the wide, flattish bowl – ideal for everyday food such as pasta, meal-in-one salads and big, warming soups. Look out for an everyday service that includes this invaluable item, which may be billed as a traditional soup plate or a small serving bowl.

Store everyday china near the table for easy laying, and at a height where younger members of the household can reach it to help (once they are old enough), or near the dishwasher if you prefer. Open shelves provide easiest access, but they don't protect the china from dust and grease – this is not a problem if it is regularly used and washed.

choosing
cutlery

THERE ARE four main considerations when choosing cutlery – the look, the feel, the type and quality of material from which it is made, and the amount of time you want to spend caring for it.

It is possible to find cutlery made of metals like brass and even gold-plate, but generally it is produced from either silver or stainless steel and comes in traditional and contemporary designs. If you like the appearance of both silver and stainless steel, the question to ask yourself is how long you want to spend caring for it. Silver is un-doubtedly more work, but you may think that the beauty of its distinctive pearly whiteness is worth the trouble. Silver is, after all, a precious metal.

Stainless steel is a popular and practical choice for cutlery today. Easy to care for, it is made in designs which straddle the centuries – some with pistol handles and three-prong forks inspired by seventeenth century silverware, others which are uncompromisingly contemporary in outline and detail, such as those designed by David Mellor, Arne Jacobsen and Georg Jensen.

The best design from any era should mix happily with the best from another, so don't feel tied to traditional style cutlery just because your china, for example, is antique. Take some of it when choosing your cutlery, or ask in advance if you

can buy a few different place settings on a sale-or-return basis, to see which looks best at home.

Always handle the cutlery, feeling its weight and balance, before buying. Beware of knives whose handles are much heavier than the blade (which is thinner and often made of different stainless steel for optimum cutting quality); a heavy-handled knife is prone to fall off the plate if balanced on the side. Knives also sometimes come with different length handles. Remember that men usually have larger hands than women, so while a short-handled knife may look more elegant and be comfortable for a woman, it could be too dainty for a man. If you eat plenty of meat, consider knives with serrated blades. If you want fish knives and forks, check that the style you choose includes these.

Stainless steel comes in different grades and finishes. The better the grade, the more expensive and long-lasting the cutlery should be. Many manufacturers offer a mirror or matt finish, the former much shinier than the latter. Mirror will show finger and other marks more readily, so matt is more practical if the cutlery is for everyday use, especially by children. Mirror, however, is considered by some to be smarter, perhaps because it resembles silver more closely.

You could keep a silver canteen, an heirloom

Elegant contemporary stainless steel cutlery created by Swedish designer Vivianna Torun Bülow-Hübe (main picture, above) who also designed the top pair of salad servers in the picture opposite. The lower pair is by Arne Jacobsen, who made butterfly and ant chairs famous. Silverware does not have to follow classical Georgian or Victorian lines. This ornate setting (inset, right) was created in 1915 by Dane Johan Rohde but is still available today through Georg Jensen.

perhaps, for special occasions only, using stainless steel for everyday meals. This certainly reduces the time spent caring for the silver, as it lies most of the time unused in the dark. If you want silver cutlery for day to day use, one solution is to buy

an old plated service cheaply from a junk shop and clean it using the aluminium method described in Caring for Cutlery on page 121. This saves work, and if the service was inexpensive it won't matter so much if it wears out.

racks, hooks and trolleys

NO MATTER how ruthless you are about clearing out clutter there are countless essential items that must be housed in any cook's kitchen; small gadgets, tools, aprons, mittens, oven gloves, tea towels – all need a place to 'live' between uses. Yet more items should be handy without clogging the place up – red wine adjusting to room temperature, for example, bulbs of garlic or favourite kitchen knives. To keep all these objects orderly and available, look at the range of storage ideas offered by retailers, or construct your own. The most versatile of these are hooks, racks and trolleys.

The hook, that simple piece of curved material, is a wonderful thing and a kitchen, especially a living kitchen, can hardly have enough of them. Not only can they be attached to the wall or the sides of furniture, they can also be screwed into the undersides of shelves (cuphooks for hanging up mugs, cups and jugs) or hung from a rail or rack. Hooks and a rail can hold lightweight items like colanders, sieves,

ladles, large serving or slotted spoons and small pans (look out for ones with a hole in the handle).

The hook can also hold more bulky (but still fairly light) items – hang see-through nylon or string net bags full of children's kitchen kit or playdough equipment, freezer boxes or plastic carrier bags awaiting re-use, or cans waiting to be recycled.

Racks, meanwhile, are designed for many purposes, from storing wine and other bottles to keeping pan lids tidy, or creating an extra layer of storage for dry goods or cans between the existing shelves of a cupboard. Use them to keep order inside cupboards and on the wall for visible items.

Gone are the days of the fancy gilt metal or plastic trolley from which the hostess served dainty cups of tea. Trolleys for the living kitchen are sturdy constructions of wood and/or stainless steel or chrome and come in a variety of sizes, heights and combinations. Some have a thick, wooden top for use like a butcher's block or

chopping board; some have a wine rack below; others have pull-out metal or wicker baskets for vegetables or a segmented tray for cutlery. A large, solid trolley can add extra worksurface or storage from day to day and can be used as a

sideboard or serving table for larger meals. Remember, though, that the great asset of a trolley is its versatility and manoeuvrability – a trolley that is too heavy or awkward to push does not fulfil its function.

These items of furniture and fittings are incomparably useful in the living kitchen, allowing flexibility and adding storage. They can also be decorative, as this simple, lengthy rail (above) demonstrates. Not only are the more predictable cooking implements and mugs hung from it with hooks, but it also supports a shelf for jars and a rack for rolls of paper towel, foil and film. This trolley (left) incorporates a hefty chopping board and drawers; other designs have baskets for fresh vegetables, a bottle rack or other useful storage devices. The wire rack (far left) can also store vegetables or, as here, cleaning kit such as cotton dishcloths. A Shaker style kitchen has a peg rail (opposite above) for chopping boards and a blackboard, while a wood and wire rack (opposite below) dries plates.

art and artefacts

THE WALLS of a living kitchen are much like those in any other room in that they call out for decoration, either with colour alone or with the addition of art or artefacts. The kitchen is the ideal place to display objects with a culinary connection, such as china, antique utensils or decorative product packaging. Well away from the steamy area around the cooker and sink, there is no reason why you should not also hang art works.

decorative china

Plates of various sizes, including large serving platters, seem appropriate for a kitchen, so look out for decorative but inexpensive examples. They can be hung in rows or other arrangements; smaller plates around one larger one, perhaps. There are two traditional methods of hanging plates. The first is a wire plate-hanger which grips the china at the top and bottom and is fixed by a nail in the wall. Less obtrusive is the second type of plate-hanger – an adhesive plastic disc that sticks to the back of the china (without damaging it, and it can be removed later by soaking).

The traditional way of displaying (and at the same time storing) china was on a plate rack, a narrow shelf which ran around the top of the room and had a groove or moulding to prevent the china slipping off. Something similar can be made today by your joiner, or a similar effect can be achieved by using small shelves on the wall. Or simply balance each plate on a couple of nails hammered into the wall or a beam if this arrangement is secure.

other ideas

Pans and antique kitchen utensils like ladles or whisks should be hung in a pattern, either a row of ascending size, or something more ingenious (but if in doubt, keep it simple). If you have an empty wall, hang one large piece on it for effect – anything from a painting or poster to an ethnic textile, or make a large, brightly coloured pinboard on which to display a changing pageant of your children's art. You can even hang children's paintings and pictures by pegging them to a 'washing' line strung across the room.

An old-fashioned kitchen artefact like the one opposite can be a source of puzzlement as well as fascination. What does it do? Is it a cheese press? Or a small butter churn? In fact it is a knife cleaner. You insert the blades of your knives in the slots around the edge and turn the handle. If you have old steel-bladed knives, there's no reason why a gadget like this cannot continue to work for you today if its insides are in good order.

rugs, floorcloths and doormats

RUGS CAN be a great decorating asset in a living kitchen, as long as they are practical and hygienic. Throughout the kitchen use them to denote different areas of the room for different activities – a luxurious rug in front of a sofa, for example, adds warmth and comfort for relaxation, and is soft for children playing on the floor. The dining area can be marked out by a rug, so long as it is big enough; one that is too small will be caught around the edges by the legs of chairs which won't do it any good, and may cause accidents.

Practicality and hygiene are particularly important in the cooking area where a little comfort underfoot can be added if you find that a hard floor (such as terracotta, quarry or other tiles, terrazzo or flagstones) tires your feet. Sheepskin and other long fibres are not recommended. In the cooking area the rug should be washable, or at least shakeable (rush matting, for example), and not so valuable that it cannot be thrown out when past its best. It must lie flat, so that it does not trip anyone up, and it must stay put – a sheet of gripper laid underneath will prevent it sliding around.

Floorcloths are another practical floorcovering, and were popular for hundreds of years before the advent of modern floorings. A floorcloth is, literally, a painted cloth for use like a mat on the floor. You can make one yourself, by priming and then painting sturdy cotton canvas (with household primer and paint), and finishing it with several coats of varnish. The advantage of a floorcloth, besides being washable and hardwearing, is that it can be made in any size, shape and pattern and, like a rug, will introduce a splash of colour to the decorative scheme.

Finally, the doormat. If you have a door opening directly from the kitchen to the terrace or garden (the ideal living kitchen has one) it is vital to use a doormat of some description to limit the dust and dirt brought in onto the kitchen floor. The traditional, tufty brown type comes in a range of colours and designs. A simple washable woven cotton mat or small rug is another option, providing it will not slip about or ruck up into folds.

The most useful types of doormat are either tough and tufty like the one below middle, or easily washable like the cotton mats (opposite, below right and below left). These are all small enough to put in a washing machine, are colourful and patterned so that they make a contribution to the look of the kitchen, and are not so precious that they can't be discarded when they become threadbare. They can also be used in front of a cooker or sink to ease the workers' feet (provided they stay flat). A wool rug like this (above left) adds a touch of luxury to the sitting or dining area of a living kitchen, while these elegant rugs made from natural plant fibres (above right) edged with coloured cotton webbing can be well shaken out of doors to keep them clean.

Simple white cotton covers like these (left) transform your everyday chairs into something special for a lunch or dinner party. Be sure to shrink the fabric by washing it thoroughly before making up the covers.

Cushions covered in pretty patterned fabrics (right) soften the lines of a bergere sofa in the seating area of a spacious country living kitchen. The same colours are picked out by plain fabrics on other chairs in the room.

chair cushions and covers

CHAIR CUSHIONS and covers, and some window treatments (see page 104), can introduce fabric other than table linen into the kitchen. Certain materials are more suitable than others – washable ones obviously being the most practical. Of course more unusual and valuable fabrics can be used, perhaps as cushions on chair seats and a sofa or comfortable chair, provided you are prepared to dry clean them from time to time and can protect them from the ministrations of small children.

Cushions on the seats of chairs tend to slide about, and onto the floor, unless they are attached, and often the ties on ready-made seat cushions are hopelessly inadequate. They must be generously long, so that a strong bow can be tied around the chair, and firmly attached to the cushion, or they will rip off easily. You can replace the ties of shop-bought cushions with strong ribbons in a matching or contrasting colour, or create a more tailored look with 'ties' which

actually button over or close, apparently seamlessly, with the aid of Velcro or press studs. Alternatively, forget ties altogether and simply sew a square of 'gripper' fabric onto the bottom of the cushion.

Loose covers are useful for dressing up dining chairs for special occasions or to mark the changes of the seasons. Choose an outline that is tailored and streamlined rather than frilled or elaborate, to prevent it dating, and use a fabric that fits into the room's overall scheme. A washable material will save time and money, and consider reinforcing the seats of the covers as this is where they will get most wear.

A comfortable chair or sofa in the kitchen should be covered either in an eminently wipe clean fabric in a forgiving colour or, better still, loose covers that can be removed and washed. A patterned fabric or one with a patterned weave will disguise small marks better than a plain one, and a strong or rich colour better than a pale one.

Seat cushions for chairs around the table (right, above and below) **should have long sturdy ties, if they are to attach to the chair, and removable, washable covers. This cushion** (right, below) **makes a decorative virtue of its cover fastening which is a button in the middle of an envelope closure on the back. Contrasting edging fabric adds to its decorative appeal.**

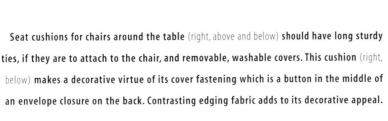

window treatments

The slats of this green-painted Venetian blind make a strongly contemporary decorating statement.

THE IDEAL living kitchen has plenty of natural daylight and sweet fresh air flooding through generously proportioned windows, including a glazed door or doors opening onto the garden or terrace. Windows are thus one of the main elements in a decorating scheme, the more so as they frame the view beyond. You don't, of course, have to dress the windows at all. If there is no need for privacy after dark (if no one else's home overlooks yours, for instance), and if double or triple glazing means there is no need for extra insulation, you may decide against blinds, shutters or any other window covering. However, some people still like to have curtains or blinds to make the room cosy and intimate after dark.

Hygiene is an important consideration when using fabric anywhere in the kitchen – acres of frilly curtain material would soon become grubby and greasy, especially around the cooking area. Curtains also take up room. For these reasons blinds are more suitable. Curtains, too (with the exception of floaty sheers and simple forms like linen panels), are less in tune than blinds with the pared down, sleek and streamlined mood of contemporary decorating.

Blinds come in a range of designs, the simplest being the roller blind, the Roman blind and Venetian blinds. You can make a roller blind yourself with a kit and your own choice of fabric, but there is a wide choice of ready-made roller blinds available from stores and by mail-order.

Roman blinds are elegant and handsome, but need sufficient space above the window to accommodate the deep folds of fabric when the blind is drawn up. They are also relatively heavy, which means that a wide window might need two or more separate blinds. Venetian blinds with their horizontal slats are available in many finishes and colours. Though they have a reputation of being fiddly to keep clean, they are undoubtedly sleek and modern, are suitable for windows of any width and pull up into a relatively small space. The Venetian blind can also be used to retain some privacy while still letting in daylight, by having the slats half-open.

Shutters have the same appeal of unfussy simplicity. Timber shutters provide total black-out and insulation at night, while Perspex shutters are elegant and uncompromisingly modern. Shutters do not have to be fitted to the whole window – if the bottom half alone is shuttered for privacy this leaves the upper part through which to see daylight or the stars. Don't forget to allow space into which the shutters can swing

This roller blind (left) has the added interest of a pierced pattern. Two roller blinds covering adjoining windows (below) are different colours and are translucent, veiling the handsome sash windows rather than masking them totally.

when they are opened back – this means that the window sill cannot hold objects, unless you are prepared to move them every time.

A modern alternative to any window covering is to apply a finish to the window glass itself, or to use a special type of glass. Today's choice includes frosted, coloured and mirrored glass (with the mirror side outwards, obviously), and even a high-tech glass that contains particles which, when activated by the flick of an electric switch, transform transparent glass into opaque.

Sticky-back translucent coloured plastic sheeting offers wonderful possibilities for decorating windows to retain privacy – or simply for the fun of the colours. Use it in plain sheets or cut out shapes, patterns, letters or whole words. Etching spray is another option; mask your pattern with shapes cut out of sticky-back

plastic, apply the spray then peel back the plastic to reveal small areas of clear glass. Such effects, which veil the window rather than shutting out light completely, can conceal a less-than-attractive view while blocking little light, if any.

Another way of veiling rather than shutting out a view is with a bead curtain, or one made of shells, pebbles, conkers, bits of broken coloured glass, discarded CDs or anything else that can be attached to strings and hung over the window. This is a useful replacement for a door, too, in sites where you want easy access but don't want the view through – from a living kitchen into a utility room, for example. Bright, colourful, cheap plastic versions can be bought ready-made.

If you want curtains, they can be sheer and floaty when insulation is not an issue. If the aim is to prevent draughts, the curtain must be more substantial (interlining will do the job best), should cover the window or door completely, and if full length, should drape onto the floor, or at least brush its surface. Alternative window drapes include rugs, throws and other ready-finished textile panels such as bedspreads and blankets. For an almost-instant curtain heading, either fold the top over (making the most of decorative borders or fringes) and sew a channel for a pole, or attach tabs from which it can be hung. Or use curtain rings which have sturdy clips to grip the top of the fabric securely. Holes can be punched along the folded-over top and reinforced with metal eyes (you can buy these as a kit), then hang the curtain from a slender metal rod or a wire.

Well away from the cooking area where their folds might absorb grease and steam, these cheerful cotton curtains (opposite) use a generous amount of fabric. They hang from above the window to well below the sill, blocking out draughts after dark.

Tall, painted shutters are the perfect window treatment in this plain Shaker style kitchen (above). When they fit properly, timber shutters provide sound and heat insulation and are elegant and restrained. If you have an old house you may find the originals nailed into the recess to each side of a window, if you are lucky. If the shutters have been removed in a previous 'modernisation', employ a joiner to make new ones for you. A smartly folding Roman blind such as this one (right) made from a luxuriously heavy, slubbed fabric, is a handsome alternative to shutters.

everyday
table linen

LIKE EVERYDAY china, table linen (such as napkins and tablecloths) that is used frequently takes quite a hammering and needs to be either hardwearing or easily replaced. It can also be less formal in design and colour. To do its job well it should be made from natural fibres, cotton and linen being the most absorbent and pleasant to the touch. Napkins are, after all, one of the few items of household linen that actually come into contact with your face.

cheerful ideas

Here follow some ideas for cheerful everyday table linen:

- Brightly checked seersucker (doesn't need ironing), matching or in various colours
- Brightly coloured napkins in one design but several different colours
- Napkins of the same design and colour (rotate them regularly so that some don't fade more than others)
- Napkins in various patterns and sizes but with a colour theme linking them (classic blue and white, for example, or floral patterns)
- Napkins around 40cm (roughly 16in) square – big enough to be practical but you don't have acres of fabric to wash
- Fabric mats big enough to lay a setting's cutlery on them – the same colour or two or more colours around the table
- Cloths which are the same shape as the table (square, rectangular or round) and hang down at least 30cm (12in) all round
- Plastic-coated cloth in cheerful colours and patterns for everyday use with children
- Other coloured tablecloths to go over the plastic one – seersucker is again ideal because it doesn't require ironing
- Cloth and napkins which match in colour and pattern
- Provençal printed cotton napkins and tablecloth in saturated colours like mustard yellow and cerulean blue
- Furnishing fabric sample pieces or remnants, hemmed or fringed (run round with the machine to prevent the fringe fraying) for napkins, sewn together in big patchwork squares for the cloth.

Everyday table linen can be brightly coloured (opposite and above, top picture), or you can arrange napkins of two or more colours at intervals around the table. Table cloths and napkins can have a pattern, be embroidered, fringed (as opposite) or made from fabric with an interesting weave like these waffle-woven napkins (above, lower picture).

special
occasion table linen

TABLE LINEN makes an important contribution to the appearance of the table laid for a special occasion. Most impressive of all is traditional, heavy, white linen damask; the cloth gleams, its satin weave polished by the pressure of the steam iron, napkins lie or stand by each place, self-consciously bulky. There is something magnificently sacrificial about so much white fabric waiting to be assaulted by red wine and gravy, mayonnaise and lipstick.

Special occasion table linen does not have to be white, but white is uniquely glamorous, because of its snowy dazzle and impracticality. Often it is pure linen, as this remarkable fibre is so covetable. Not only is it expensive, handsome and hardwearing but it is also highly absorbent, and dries quickly after washing. Linen takes dye well too; a mildly stained cloth

found, say, in a junk shop can be transformed with some dye and a swirl in the washing machine.

A dinner party or a Sunday lunch with guests is an opportunity to give special table linen an airing. A very fine cloth may need another underneath it for support, and perhaps a rug or blanket under this (but hidden) to give the table added luxurious softness and smoothness. This bottom layer is essential if the table has any rough corners or edges.

If your treasured cloth has white-on-white (or indeed coloured) embroidery, or drawn threadwork, an undercloth in a plain bright or strong colour can throw the decoration into relief. The colour of the undercloth could be picked up elsewhere on the table, in flowers or coloured napkins for example, or it could echo a colour on the china or the kitchen decorations.

Table linen for special occasions was traditionally heavy and white, carefully stored out of the light and dust to emerge pristine for feasts and celebrations. White linen still exerts a special fascination, but there is no reason why coloured table linen should not be used for special occasions; indeed, it could be said to be more festive. If you use coloured napkins, take the trouble to link the tones with other items on the table – flowers, for example – for a unified, themed appearance. Every guest can have a napkin and perhaps a table mat of the same colour, or alternatively you could vary these around the table which will give a joyful, carnival look and help create the right atmosphere for a party.

candles and scents

A steep-sided black lacquer Japanese bowl with tiny white candles and bright pink nerine blossoms floating in it makes a dramatic centrepiece.

CANDLELIGHT HAS been considered flattering and romantic for centuries. For most of this time it was essential for evening activities and entertaining, but its appeal has lasted long since the advent of electric power. Today, there is more choice than ever in the shape, size and colour of candles and their holders – there are even candles with scented wax. A small burner for scented oils is another way of giving a room the heady smell of citrus fruits, jasmine or bergamot.

When planning candles for the table, remember that a tall candelabra holding several candles may block the sightlines of the people sitting around it. This matters less if the table is wide or if the candleholder is delicate. Alternatives include a row of smaller candlesticks along the table, a low candle arrangement, or clusters of tapers standing in jars of sand or salt. A low arrangement could comprise floating candles and flower heads in a wide, shallow bowl of (possibly scented) water, or tea lights in a ceramic or metal holder designed for the job. Tea lights also look charming in small coloured glass holders, antique pressed glasses or containers with a mosaic of coloured glass pieces glued to the sides. You can make the last at home, using craft clay, grout or plaster to fill the gaps between the pieces for a smooth finish.

The perfect site for other candles is a mantelshelf across a fireplace. Window sills, too, offer space for candles, the dancing light reflecting in the glass. Candles can be placed on a counter top, sideboard or on shelving, but always be aware of the dangers of damage and fire; never let candles burn low or leave them burning unattended.

Scents hanging in the air add immeasurably to atmosphere, be they the spices, garlic or chocolate that have gone into the evening's meal, or other more unusual and elusive aromas. Scented candles can provide exotic perfumes, as can an oil burner. This is usually a small china container with two tiers: a tea light is placed in the lower tier while a small quantity of scented oil (or your own mixture of sweet almond oil and essential oil) is poured into an indentation in the upper part. As the candle heats the container, the scent is released from the warm oil. Essential oils can also pep up bowls of lavender flowers or pot pourri. In summer, though, there is no prettier way of bringing sweet scents into the home than with a bunch of garden-fresh flowers and herbs.

Pretty egg-shaped glass oil burners (above) contain scented oil whose tones subtly pervade the air during the course of the evening. Simple wax tapers (right) have been pushed into jars of ordinary cooking salt in earthenware flower pots and a square aluminium planter.

CHAPTER FIVE

THE TABLE

THIS CHAPTER EASES THE WAY TO CAREFREE ENTERTAINING. IT SUGGESTS HOW TO LAY A TABLE, HOW TO CHOOSE TABLE LINEN FOR EVERY DAY AND FOR SPECIAL OCCASIONS, AND HOW TO LOOK AFTER IT. HERE YOU CAN FIND PRACTICAL TIPS ON MAKING GLASS, STAINLESS STEEL OR SILVER SPARKLE AND IDEAS FOR SEASONAL TABLE DECORATIONS INCLUDING FRUIT, FLOWERS, SHELLS AND AUTUMN LEAVES.

DO YOU often wonder if you should have a table plan, or simply let everyone sit where they want? If you do decide on a seating plan, or *placement*, how do you mark each person's place – with a plain but handsome name card, or with something a little more individual? There used to be a traditional way of setting a table, but is it still necessary to stick to such routine? This chapter gives a list of ideas you might need to ensure that you are not forever jumping up to fetch things while you are entertaining.

Sitting down to an uninterrupted meal with family and friends, with delicious things to eat and drink, is one of life's great pleasures, but there is always the tricky issue of serving up and clearing away. Now that the age of the separate dining room has passed, we have to think up new and ingenious ways of hiding the clutter of preparation as well as the ongoing detritus of a meal in progress. Read on for some practical ways to minimize the guests' view of piles of serving bowls and dirty dishes.

laying the table

Laying the table (above) **is the most important preparation before your guests arrive. A well-laid table will make them feel welcome, even if you are running late. There is wonderfully colourful paper tableware available for events involving children** (opposite)**; the guiding rule here is generally the brighter the better.**

THE ONLY vital task to complete before your guests arrive is to lay the table. Never mind if you haven't unpacked the shopping or started cooking. If the table is laid, the glass sparkling and the linen smooth, your friends will know that they are welcome and their appetites will be whetted for the evening (or lunchtime) ahead. They can always chat to you while you prepare the meal – this is, after all, a living kitchen.

Before laying a table, think of the actual table first. Clear it, then clean it thoroughly. If using a cloth or mats, or both (mats under the cloth to protect the table from hot plates) lay these in position, then place large items like candle-sticks and flower, fruit or vegetable arrangements down the middle. Add cutlery – everything each person will need, and any necessary serving spoons – and items like table napkins and place cards. Next come drinking glasses, and finally, all the little extras like (well-filled) salt and pepper grinders, relishes and sauces, coasters for wine bottles (and perhaps the wine itself, if it is red) and jugs or bottles of water.

The correct arrangement of cutlery has taxed writers on etiquette for generations. Today, realistically, only a stuffy person is going to care if you get it 'wrong'. The main consideration is that a guest is comfortable because he or she has every tool they need for eating. The same applies to special implements for special food. A long narrow fork is undoubtedly useful for teasing the meat out of a lobster, but fish knives and forks are fading out in all but grand or traditional households, as are fruit knives and forks. On the other hand, if you already possess such things – heirlooms, perhaps – and want to use them, then why not?

A guideline for laying cutlery is as follows: work from the outside in, which is to say that the cutlery with which your guests will eat their first course is placed furthest away from the mat or plate. A small knife used to eat bread off a small plate placed to the side (possibly used again later for cheese) goes furthest of all, on the right. The blades of knives lie with the sharp edge facing the mat. Pudding spoon and fork are placed either to right and left of the mat or above it (more practical, leaving room between each person's place, and more appealing visually).

There is nothing more annoying, for host and guests, than having to get up from the table at intervals to collect something that has been forgotten. So here is a list of items you may need, to help you lay the perfect table:

- Mat for each place and others, if needed, in the middle of the table for serving bowls
- Cloth
- Cutlery for each course

- Knife for eating bread and butter, and cheese, off a side plate
- Large serving implements for vegetables or salad
- Small or special serving spoons for relishes, pickles, gravy, croutons, parmesan etc
- Glass(es) for wine
- Water glass
- Coaster(s) for wine bottles
- Water bottles or jugs
- Side plate to the left of each place
- Napkin folded on each side plate
- Place card with the guest's name
- Butter on dish(es)
- Butter knife or knives
- Salt grinder(s) or dish(es) and pepper grinder(s) – well-filled
- Mustard, grated cheese for sprinkling, extra croutons, jelly, dressing, gravy or other sauces/relishes
- Toothpicks in a small bowl or jar
- Finger bowls containing warm water and slices of lemon, if serving a messy dish eaten with fingers
- Discard bowls – for the empty shells of mussels, for example
- Special items for children
- Decorative elements like candles, flowers, fruit, vegetables, shells etc.

Other items to have ready at the side:
- heated plates for all hot courses
- cold plates for separate salad or cheese
- pudding bowls or plates
- sweet biscuits or sauces to serve with pudding (remove all savoury pickles etc when placing sweet ones on the table)
- celery or salad, bread or biscuits to serve with cheese

caring for
pure linen

NOTHING COMPARES with the luxury of natural cloth and in particular pure linen. Produced from fibres derived from flax, linen is a wonderfully hardwearing and absorbent fabric, making it ideal for use at table.

Not only does pure linen look wonderful, with its dense, matt finish, but it is also, contrary to popular belief, easy to care for. Not for linen the gentle cycle in the machine or time-consuming washing by hand (unless, of course, you have delicate, very fine or antique pieces) – linen can generally be washed on a hot cycle, up to ninety degrees centigrade. If your napkins and cloth have food or other stains, drop them into a bucket of pre-soak solution straight after the meal and leave for several hours before washing. Put all matching linen in the bucket, even if some of it is clean, so that every piece is exactly the same colour after washing. Be prepared for shrinkage and colour loss when hotwashing new linen for the first time – after this there should be no shrinkage and only gradual colour fading over time.

Once washed, take the linen out of the machine as soon as the programme has finished, if possible, to limit crumpling. Hang it on the line or dryer so that each piece is square – don't be tempted to save space by pegging napkins up by the corner as this will distort their shape. Get each piece as square and wrinkle-free as possible by shaking and pulling it. Embroidery and lace, especially around the edges, should be gently stretched so that it doesn't dry puckered. A useful tip for fitting many napkins on an airing rack indoors is to hang each one on a wire hanger – that way more will fit on one rail.

In theory, you should whip linen off the line when it is still slightly damp and iron it immediately, but who in reality has the time or patience for that? Instead, thoroughly dampen the linen before ironing with a handheld household mister, or use an efficient steam iron on a hot setting. Using lavender or rose water will make the napkins smell delicious but check the manufacturer's recommendations before putting it in an iron. Linen can be starched for extra stiffness and sophistication, either with shop-bought starch or naturally by dipping each piece in water drained from cooked white rice.

Of course it doesn't have to be ironed at all if you are happy with the natural, rough and slightly crumpled look it has after washing. Most people, however, love the flat, silky smoothness of the ironed finish.

A steam iron provides the easiest method of producing that crisp, smooth finish we all love.

Nothing compares with the feel on one's hands and face of real, pure linen table napkins (left). Cool linen looks as much at home as part of the simple set up here as it does at a grand and splendid table.

We think of silver as being labour-intensive to care for, but there are ways of limiting the work involved if you really love the pearly beauty of this precious metal. Keep cutlery and other pieces out of the light, ideally in airtight bags or ones impregnated with anti-tarnish chemicals. Alternatively, take pride in a display of your silver, especially if you have heirlooms, and learn to enjoy the relaxing rhythm of silver polishing. Stainless steel is less trouble but also repays some care and attention. It is dishwasher proof but often benefits from a rub with a soft cloth after it has dried. Never leave either silver or stainless steel to soak in water.

caring for silver and stainless steel cutlery

AT A glance, the difference between stainless steel and silver cutlery is that the former is carefree whilst the latter is a lot of bother. While it's true that stainless steel is easier to look after, some care is needed – and it is also true that there are ways of keeping down the maintenance involved in caring for silver.

The quickest way of cleaning silver is to fill a basin with warm water, dissolve soda crystals in it, then place aluminium foil or bottle tops in the mixture. When silver is placed in this solution, a chemical reaction takes place which transforms it before your eyes. The time it takes to remove the tarnish depends on the strength of the solution and the condition of the cutlery, so keep an eye on it and be ready to take it out when appropriate, then rinse and dry it thoroughly. Store silver out of the light, ideally in cloth bags designed for the job. These have a slot for each piece, and some are made from fabric impregnated with a chemical that helps prevent tarnishing.

Knives with wooden or bone handles (and many with mock bone – check with the manufacturer) should not be cleaned in the dishwasher as the heat melts and swells the glue which makes the handles drop out (and the dishwasher does the wood or bone no good).

No cutlery should be left soaking in water, not even stainless steel; tap water contains small amounts of dissolved mineral salts, and prolonged immersion in water can cause corrosion. Many foods are corrosive, too, or can cause stains (salt, vinegars, lemon, hot fat in particular) as are other materials like bleach and very hard water. Sulphides tarnish silver, and these are not only in the air but also in some foods, notably eggs. Rainbow stains can appear on stainless steel if there is a film of strong detergent, or if it has become extremely hot. A rinse and polish should remove them.

The simple rule for all cutlery is to clean it as soon after use as possible and dry it properly after that. Don't soak it, and do occasionally give it a buff with a soft cloth. Silver will occasionally need to be polished with an impregnated cloth or with a paste, or by being dipped. Be careful to use only products specifically for silver, follow the instructions and use only the minimum effective quantity, as cleaners can do harm as well as good. Don't leave even tiny amounts of paste on the silver (highly decorated and pierced items are particularly at risk) because of the danger of corrosion.

caring for
glass and crystal

THERE IS something alluring about a table laid for a meal that has not yet begun, a sense of incompleteness, an air of anticipation. People, food and drink are needed to complete the scene, with warmth and the sound of conversation and laughter. But until they arrive, the table presents a tableau of smooth linen, gleaming china and cutlery, glittering glassware. The effect is even more magical in sunshine or candlelight, the sparkle of glasses waiting for wine or water providing the only movement other than motes of dust dancing in the beams.

Glassware falls into two distinct categories: everyday glass and lead crystal. The distinction lies in the lead content of the material. To deserve its name, full lead crystal must consist of at least thirty per cent lead. This gives a material that sparkles brilliantly because of the way in which it refracts light, and is heavier and more satisfying to handle. Crystal glassware is made in contemporary styles as well as the familiar, traditional cut-glass designs.

Most glassware can be cleaned in the dishwasher but may occasionally need an extra rinse and polish by hand with a clean cotton cloth. If you do use a dishwasher don't cram glasses together, as they may break in the heat (and don't stack tumblers that are fresh and hot from the dishwasher as they may shatter when they cool and shrink slightly). When removing glasses from the dishwasher, handle only the stem of wine glasses and the sides near the base of tumblers, to avoid leaving finger marks.

Lead crystal can be washed in the dishwasher on a medium cycle without detergent powder, but most people prefer to wash it by hand to prevent it developing a milky white 'clouding'. Always rinse after washing and before drying, otherwise the tang of soap residue will spoil the taste of the next drink from the glass.

Cleaning decanters through the neck can be problematic. If a bottle brush doesn't work, try filling the decanter with cool, fresh water and drop into this chunks of raw, peeled potato. This traditional method helps remove marks from glass jugs too. To dry the decanter, use a special shot-filled cotton bag, long and narrow in shape, which will snake round the bottom while you twist the end sticking out from the neck. If all else fails, crystal decanters and jugs can be sent away for professional cleaning. And, if you are unlucky enough to chip a crystal glass or decanter lip, specialists can mend the damage by grinding down the edges.

These fine-stemmed wine glasses (main picture, above) have been washed by hand in hot, soapy water (near left, middle and bottom), rinsed well to remove all traces of detergent, and are drying in a rack awaiting a final wipe with a clean, dry cotton or linen cloth. This decanter (near left, top) is being cleaned by chunks of raw potato in cool water — one of many old-fashioned, chemical-free methods of maintaining tableware. A folding wooden rack (far left) is handy for drying hand-washed bone china or glasses of all sorts; it can be folded flat and hidden in a cupboard afterwards.

fresh flowers

FRESH FLOWERS on the table have a special appeal because they are… fresh. Plastic flowers can be fun and kitsch, silk flowers are sophisticated and astonish with their deception, dried flowers tend to be dead and dusty – there is simply nothing to compare with the colour, texture and immediacy of freshly cut flowers, their beauty all the more poignant because they do not last for ever.

If you are in doubt about your flower-arranging abilities, keep it simple. A generous bundle of tulips in a straight-sided glass vase look ravishing and so much better than a tortured attempt at something more 'professional'. Single flowers in a row of jars look stylish, as do flower heads floating in a shallow bowl of scented water.

To let flowers speak for themselves, use a plain, sophisticated container. For extra interest, place coloured glass or plain grey pebbles and shells in the bottom of a glass vase before adding the water and flowers. Country flowers, however, look pretty in old, patterned jugs. If you are short of vases, simply wrap brown or coloured paper around a plain jar, tying it with raffia or contrasting coloured ribbon.

To make the most of fresh flowers, cut an inch or two off the stems and stand them in a bucket of tepid water, in a cool place, for a couple of hours at least but preferably overnight, before you start arranging.

Then, giving yourself plenty of space in which to work, remove the wrapping carefully so that you handle the flowers as little as possible. Cut the bottoms off the stems with sharp scissors and remove all foliage that will lie below the waterline, and any other foliage that is damaged or faded. Cut the stalks down in proportion with the size of the flowers themselves, and of the vase – tall, straggly blooms in a small container look daft. Add contrasting greenery for a more verdant look.

Searing the stems of almost any flowering plant can extend their vase life considerably. To do this, pour a couple of inches of boiling water into a container and simply stand the flowers in this for less than a minute, protecting the heads from any steam. This works better than crushing the ends of woody stalks such as roses.

Once the flowers are trimmed, three-quarters fill the vase with tepid water and flower food before placing the flowers in it. Either buy sachets of flower food or make your own by adding a teaspoon each of sugar, vinegar (white or pale in a glass vase) and bleach. During the life of the flowers replace the water regularly. The stalks can be cut down further and seared again to extend the flowers' life.

For a magical table arrangement combining fresh produce with flickering candlelight (left), cut a piece out of a bright red or green apple and sit a tea light in the hole. If any of the flesh of the fruit is exposed, paint this with lemon juice before inserting the candle to prevent it turning brown during the meal. Pebbles, limes and leaves (opposite, above) are an unexpected combination that lends a touch of visual drama to the table, while a Zen-like arrangement of pebbles and beautiful dishes (opposite, below) is restrained and calm.

other table
arrangements

IT IS not only fresh flowers that can make a stunning table centrepiece – foliage, fruit, vegetables, pebbles and shells are contemporary alternatives. The variety of colours, textures and forms in foliage alone, without flowers, can create an impressive arrangement – to get the best from greenery, follow the guidelines described above for flowers.

The vibrant colours and glossy skins of lemons, limes, oranges and apples, not to mention some of the rarer exotic fruits, can make a dramatic impact when massed together. The fact that they are edible gives the arrangement an added sensuality, as do their plump forms and suggestion of fecundity. Grapes refer to wine and hint at bacchanalian liberty. A pineapple adds scale and drama, with its jagged, show-off headdress and rough, scaly skin.

Plumply polished aubergines and the deep-green froth of heads of broccoli, to name but two vegetables, are equally beautiful though less suggestive perhaps, because they generally have to be cooked before being truly delicious. Whatever you choose, pile the fruit or vegetables up in a wooden bowl or a basket made from wire or wicker, with an eye to the overall composition of the arrangement. Groups of fruit or vegetables often look better than individuals dotted about. Fruit can be wired in place if necessary, though this seems a shame as you may not be able to eat it later.

For a more low-key, Zen-like arrangement, spread smoothly shaped pebbles in descending size in a line, a sensuous wiggle or a satisfying spiral on the surface of the table. Shells and pebbles placed in a glass jar or shallow dish are another alternative, as are pine cones, autumn leaves and decorative twigs. Feathers and dried flowers are best avoided because of their association with dead things.

the seating plan

WITH SO much to prepare for a meal, it is easy to forget the question of whom is to sit where when the time comes to eat. And, indeed, you might ask yourself if there is any point these days in making a seating plan or *placement*. If you really don't mind where anybody sits, then the answer is no. And there are some meals, a family Sunday lunch party outdoors on a balmy summer's day, for example, when the blissful informality of the moment might be marred by over-organisation, especially if there are children involved.

On other occasions, however, a seating plan is useful for helping to make the meal a success. There are several factors to consider, including the position of the table, the type of seating and the extent to which the people present know each other.

The first decision is where you and any other hosts are to sit. This need not be at the ends of the table, though if you don't sit there, the people at the ends may feel out on a limb. The person cooking usually sits where they can easily move to serve up. Traditionally, the most honoured female guest sits on the right of the man of the house and their partner or the most distinguished male guest on the hostess's right. Etiquette also allows engaged couples to sit next to each other, but otherwise couples are separated, with male and female alternating around the table.

Local practices vary these rules from country to country. In some places couples usually sit together, so if you have visitors from abroad, a discreet enquiry in advance will help you ensure your guests feel relaxed.

Today, etiquette can be a useful guide, but you should have no compunction about seating men next to men and women next to women, or about breaking any other of the so-called 'rules' if the result is a happy *placement*. The aim is to seat each person next to someone whose company they will enjoy (including, not surprisingly, their own spouse).

There are other considerations. You will obviously want everyone to be comfortable, so an unusually tall person should sit in a position where they can stretch their legs a little, while a wheelchair or highchair needs extra space. Children can happily be crammed onto a bench, but adults need more room. Your most honoured guest should, perhaps, enjoy the best view through the window. Children often mind terribly about whom they sit next to or don't, be it a favourite cousin or godfather, or another child who is currently anathema to them. A shy person should be near one of the hosts, whilst a noisy or talkative guest can act as a focus further away. The perfect *placement* satisfies everyone and pleases you, too.

Is the seating plan an anachronism in the relaxed, informal, living kitchen? Not necessarily. It enables you to ensure that people have the opportunity to meet and talk properly, that anyone with special needs is comfortable, that children's behaviour can be restrained or unrestrained, and that the most important guest has the best view. These place-card holders (opposite) are actually freestanding clips designed to hold individual postcards, photographs or . . . anything.

Look around for decorative items that can be used to mark your guests' places at a party or special occasion. These glittery pears (left) are actually Christmas-tree decorations. Simply write the person's name on the leaf with a silver or gold metallic pen.

place cards

PLACE CARDS are useful for special occasions, or where there is a large number to seat. They can also make a delightful contribution to the appearance of the table at any occasion where there is more than the usual household complement present and where there is a seating plan to put into operation. Place cards are also uniquely practical – each person can see where they are to sit without the clumsy necessity for you or someone else to point and call out names.

Some specialist stationers keep packs of ready-printed decorated place cards for sale, but if you have time you can make your own. To do so either cut out rectangles from sheets of card, or buy some plain white record cards. These are generally around 150 x100mm (6 x 4in) and can be bought from office stationers. Fold one in half for an instant place card, just waiting for the name of the person and perhaps some decoration. Have a good pen for the job of writing names, or keep a set of coloured pens or pencils for the task if you are artistic. Another option is to photocopy a design of your own onto sheets of card and fill in the names afterwards.

For unique customized place cards, make your own and decorate them with cut-out pictures, paper flowers, glitter or beads. Or instead of propping the card in front of the place, punch a hole in each and make a decorated wire twist with which to attach it to each person's rolled-up napkin, or tie it with a length of raffia or coloured ribbon.

Single cards with no fold can be held in front of each place by small holders. These come in many designs and materials, from elaborate antique silver to contemporary glass.

When it comes to writing place cards for the table, nothing beats the simplicity and elegance of really good quality card and a fountain pen.

serving up and clearing away

ONE OF the few disadvantages of kitchen living is the problem of clearing away during and at the end of a meal. With a dining room you take everything back to the kitchen, or simply leave the room and close the door on the mess. But what do you do about all the dirty plates, the half-eaten dishes, the pans and spoons, if you are preparing food, cooking and eating in the same room?

One useful solution is to have a cooking area in your kitchen which has a raised edge or bar along the side next to the eating area, tall enough to conceal cooking clutter and mess from people sitting at table but not so tall that it feels like a barrier to conversation. If it has a flat, heatproof surface on the top all the better, it should be wide enough to stand a dish or plate on safely, which makes it a useful passing point for food in both directions.

If you can't construct such a bar, there are still several highly practical solutions to the problem of clearing away. The key to them all is planning ahead. First, clean and put away as much of your preparation kit before guests arrive, or at least before they sit down at the table. Second, have space ready on the side onto which to put items you are clearing.

The ideal is to have a utility room off the preparation area of the kitchen, with a big sink into which to dump the unsightly stuff, and a counter for dishes of food, but most of us have to do without. Decide whether you want to open the dishwasher during the meal – a machine half-filled with dirty plates and cutlery is not attractive. However, if the occasion is informal, and if the dishwasher was empty in the first place, it is undoubtedly the best solution.

Alternatively, for more formal dinner parties when you don't want either to open the dishwasher or to sit and look at the debris, have one or more large plastic or wooden boxes with lids. Put all the dirty plates and cutlery in these and clear them out later or tomorrow. Dishes of food will just have to sit on the side. A rolling shutter or a roller blind fitted to close down over the front of the counter is another option for concealment.

One last thought. If possible, don't stack plates at the table once the meal has been eaten as it involves not only the crashing of china and cutlery but also, almost invariably, some scraping of bits – not attractive for the guests especially as it's at their eye level. Better to lift the plates from the table individually and do all the messy business on the side.

CHAPTER SIX
THE TERRACE

THE PERFECT LIVING KITCHEN HAS FRENCH WINDOWS OPENING OUT
ONTO A TERRACE, BALCONY OR ROOF GARDEN FURNISHED WITH
WELCOMING CHAIRS AND A TABLE TO EAT AT, UNDER A CANOPY OR
UMBRELLA IN HOT WEATHER. HERBS GROWING IN TUBS NEARBY
SCENT THE AIR; A FROTH OF GERANIUMS AND ROSES SWELLS FROM
TERRACOTTA POTS.

YOUR TERRACE may be stone, brick, gravel or timber
decking, the furniture made from hardwood, resin or
plastic, folding or otherwise. You might like a
hammock for dozing in, or a canopy for protection
from the blazing sun.

The following pages offer ideas and information
on all these matters, as well as some tips for container
gardening, outdoor heating, cooking and lighting.

surfaces

TO MAXIMIZE the visual size of your terrace or garden, paint the walls white or a fresh, light colour. This will define the limits of the area which can then be veiled and made more mysterious with planting. The ground surface, meanwhile, can be one of several materials, the most popular currently being decking, gravel and coloured glass chippings. The classic outdoor floorings, which never seem to date, include sandstone slabs, handmade brick, gravel (again) and even turf. The last may seem labour-intensive, but if you have the energy to look after it, or have someone to do this for you, it is incomparably soft and luxurious underfoot, especially for children. Its greenness is also a treat for the eye and a little reminder of the countryside if you live in a town or city.

Walls and boundaries can be made interesting in one of the following ways:

- Paint the walls or fence:
  - white
  - bright blue for a sea-and-sky mood
  - pastel shades for a romantic garden
  - red/yellow/orange/pink for a hot, tropical feel
- Grow climbing or rambling plants up the wall
- Plant ivy or other trailing plants in containers on top of the wall, to cascade down it
- Fix rows of wires to the wall and train (or buy) espaliered fruit trees
- Stand a full-sized arch in front of a panel of mirror to create the illusion of space beyond
- Construct steps leading up to a door fixed to the wall to lead the eye upwards and to vary the

and boundaries

height at which the plant
containers stand

- Install a water feature to act
  as a focus
- Build shelves on which to
  stand pots, possibly pre-cut
  with holes into which small
  pots will fit
- Fix a pattern of glazed tiles
  onto the boundary wall
- Create a bed around the
  perimeter supported by a low
  retaining wall, or a wall high
  enough to sit on, with a wide
  edge for just that purpose
- Plant hedge in front of
  decaying fence to take over
  when it collapses
- On a roof terrace erect screening
  to act as a windbreak as well as
  to define the boundary and
  provide privacy.

Some possible ground surfaces:

- Natural paving stones or slate
- Concrete slabs
- Brick
- Setts
- Gravel
- Coloured glass chippings
- Pebble or broken-tile mosaic
- Combination of any of the above
- Timber decking
- Turf

The perfect living kitchen has a terrace just outside, for use as an extension to the room in fine weather. The most handsome and long-lasting furniture for the terrace is still made from the traditional materials, hardwood timber (all pictures) and metal (below left), but not always in traditional designs (see opposite). If you buy new wooden furniture, check that the timber comes from a sustainable source. You can leave it outdoors all year round – as the years go by it will develop a silvery patina – giving it an optional scrub and oil each spring. Metal furniture needs occasional maintenance – either oiling to prevent rust or touching up with paint if it rusts or becomes scratched. Folding furniture (below left) can more easily be stored in winter.

furniture

THE TERRACE or small garden is an extension of the living kitchen in late spring, summer and early autumn. Like the kitchen, its furniture must be fit for the job – in other words hard-working and good-looking. And, like other furniture, it comes in a range of materials and styles. The cost varies too, with the cheapest being old inherited pieces, improvized items like stools made from tree trunks, and junk-shop furniture, painted or primed with preservative wood treatment to extend its life. More expensive pieces worth investing in include sturdy hardwood benches and tables, and traditional timber loungers. Always check that the wood is from a renewable, sustainable source when you buy the furniture.

Also consider where the furniture will live out of season or in extreme weather conditions; most furniture dripping in the winter rain is not attractive. If you don't have a shed or garage in which to store it, fold and stack the furniture out of sight, standing it on a decking tile or pallet to get it off the ground, and cover it completely with a heavy-duty waterproof tarpaulin. Tie it round securely so that the wind won't lift the edges.

There are exceptions to this. Hardwood furniture can be left out and will gradually become a mellow silvery-grey over the years (you may want to give it a scrub each spring). Metal furniture can also be left out if the paint or other coating is in good condition, and if it is decorative it will become something of a feature, a focus for the eye during the dreary winter months.

Garden furniture and useful accessories take many forms:

- Wood – if hardwood check source (see above). Give it an optional scrub in spring and rub with teak oil
- 'Rustic' furniture made from whole branches and twigs
- Painted metal
- Galvanized metal – shiny and contemporary
- Resin and plastic, often in pretty or bright colours
- Painted junk – the cheap and cheerful option, relatively short-lived

- Fold-away furniture, easier to store
- On uneven grass, a metal table with a big spike is handy – simply push it into the ground
- Lounging furniture such as sunbed or hammock
- Swing or hanging seat suspended from a tree
- Don't forget colour – not all garden furniture is brown or dark green
- In temperate climates avoid white. It looks like pub garden furniture, and quickly gets grey and tatty
- Cushions, throws and rugs soften the edges of hard benches, and can be used on the (dry) ground.

shade and planting

IF YOU live through the seemingly endless grey winter months in a temperate region you probably spend so much of the year longing for the sunshine of summer that it is difficult to believe that you will ever actually yearn for shade. But not only is shade desirable in the heat of a scorching day, it is essential to protect us from the sun's harmful rays, especially in this age of ozone depletion. What's more, some people simply don't enjoy the sun's direct heat, and would rather sit in shade. For all these needs for shade there are many options.

The simplest is to buy an umbrella and a base in which to stand it. Garden umbrellas are made from a variety of materials, the most appealing probably being bamboo and cotton canvas, and wood and cotton canvas. Check the degree of waterproofness and care requirements before buying. Alternatively, an awning can be made to cover a larger area in a (suitable) fabric of your choice. This can be rectangular or some other shape – triangular like the sail of a boat, or wedge-shaped, perhaps, to suit the terrace or garden best.

Attach it at regular intervals to hooks embedded in walls, to tree branches, or support it with strong poles. Give the edges of the awning a deep hem for extra strength, and reinforce the holes for string ties or for the ends of poles with metal eyes (these can be bought in a kit).

For particularly sunny sites, consider investing in a tiny marquee, a sort of tent with sides that can be rolled up or down according to the heat and the direction of the sun. This will also retain warmth for evening entertaining (but beware of the fire hazard if using candles), and will give added privacy.

Finally, if making medium to long-term plans for your garden, consider planting a bower or pergola. A bower is a one-sided enclosure to shelter a bench or chairs and a table, up and over which decorative and scented climbers can be grown. A pergola covers a larger area such as a terrace or the part of a terrace used for sitting, and perhaps eating. In hot countries, this is where vines are trained, their fruits being enjoyed at harvest time.

tips and ideas

- CLIMBERS can be grown from pots, including some spectacular ones like quintessentially English wisteria (train it round an umbrella-shaped support around 1.25m (4ft) tall) and exotic bougainvillaea (choose a smaller, compact variety).

- To avoid the bother and mess of growing plants from seed, send for SEEDLINGS and PLANTLETS by post from mail-order nurseries.

- Consider using WATER to create a visual focus – the sound of running water is so refreshing. It may also attract birds. The water feature could look classical, with a spout jetting water into a stone basin, or contemporary, using vertical columns of bubbling, aerated water or a sculptural mix of mirror and glass forms. A wide, shallow pool of water will reflect light into a dark garden and look serenely contemplative.

- Organize planting so that there is an abundance of luxurious foliage of different shapes and tones, then add splashes of OPULENCE with brilliantly coloured canna lilies, ceanothus, repeat-flowering roses, paeonies and poppies (staking the last two so they don't fall over). Deadhead regularly to encourage new flowering, and fill gaps in your beds with bought-in blooms still in their pots. Don't forget to water these as well as your other containers.

- Manage your terrace so that it looks appealing in WINTER as well as in summer. When the best of the year is over, move evergreens in pots into prominent positions, arranged regularly around the edge of the terrace, and have a blitz in the beds to remove all dead and straggly foliage. Clean and put away furniture before it begins to look sad or slimy. Ornaments such as statues, pebbles, shells or driftwood are even more interesting in winter than summer because there is less to look at around them.

- For easy control of WEEDS, use a sponge weeder – this has a sponge attached to the end of a tube into which the weedkiller is poured. Then simply dab at the weeds when they appear. Use a glyphosate that biodegrades in the soil. The only damage it does is to the plant as it seeps down into the roots. Don't be tempted to make the mixture strong – this will merely cauterize the top of the plant. If anything, give the weeds repeated treatments of a weak solution, and add a drop of washing-up liquid to the mixture, as the detergent helps the poison drain down into the roots.

- Introduce an element of FUN into the garden with giant metallic or rainbow-coloured plastic windmills in the flowerbeds. Or hang Chinese paper lanterns, brightly coloured streamers or kites among the branches of trees or against the wall in summer. Hammocks, too, come in bright colours as well as naturals, and are wonderfully RELAXING to lie in on a lazy, balmy day.

- Grow VEGETABLES in containers on the terrace or balcony, in the raised bed around the edge of a tiny garden or in window boxes, and up the walls of the building. Carrots' frothy fronds look pretty, runner beans can climb up through rambling roses, and some vegetables (eg ruby chard, ornamental cabbage, kohlrabi) are as eye-catching as any flowers.

- Age or MELLOW new terracotta or concrete pots and planters by painting them with liquid manure, milk or live yogurt, or watered-down emulsion paint.

- Make GARDENING easier with a long-handled fork and trowel that prevent your having to bend so low.

pots and
window boxes

ALMOST ANYTHING frostproof will make a garden container for your terrace, from an old teapot to a tin trunk, especially if you can drill a few holes in the bottom for drainage. Baskets and wooden containers can be used as planters, but they will rot away eventually unless placed outdoors only in dry weather. A traditional look will incorporate terracotta pots, while a contemporary scheme revels in shiny, galvanized metal planters and pots with coloured glazes. Indeed a gleaming new dustbin can support a small standard tree (underplanted with a froth of contrasting foliage, such as senecio or artemisia for extra appeal). A row of such containers creates a dramatic impact.

For a structured, architectural look, try a regimented line of clipped standards or foliage shapes, such as box pompoms, cylinders, lollipops or pyramids, in identical containers. These punctuate the terrace so that it looks tidy and organized, while leaving room in between for more anarchic planting. For a 'jungle' effect, plant containers of different sizes and materials with a variety of plants and foliage and arrange these in groups around the perimeter.

Window boxes, like pots, come in several materials, but they must be able to be secured to the wall or sill if necessary to prevent them falling off. Likewise, pots on a roof terrace, which must not blow over the edge. The contents of window boxes and pots dry out quicker than soil in the ground, so make sure they are regularly watered and fed. Pebbles or gravel on top of the soil will help to slow down moisture loss.

Some plants that will thrive in containers:

- **Architectural plants, eg box clipped into shapes, miniature cypresses, yuccas, cordylines, phormiums**
- **Container-grown trees including olive, eucalyptus, apple, fig**
- **Two or three layers of plant giving height and depth**
- **Grasses (these can give variety of height and colour and are easy to grow), bamboos and euphorbias**
- **Other interesting foliage including cut-leaf, purple and silver**
- **Erect flowers such as agapanthus, alliums, lilies**
- **Vegetables eg carrots, cabbages, lettuces and other salad leaves**
- **Fruit such as strawberries which drape elegantly over the edge**
- **Winter interest: pansies, primroses and polyanthus, red-stemmed dogwood, hebes, evergreen shrubs, scented shrubs, grasses such as festuca glauca and early-flowering bulbs, shrubs with berries or hips such as skimmia reevesiana and rosa rugosa.**

herbs
outdoors and in

MOST HERBS are happy growing in containers or window boxes, the great advantage of the latter being that however small your garden, you can always reach out for a handful of mint or chives to throw into your cooking. Fresh herbs make it easy to produce quick dishes that look appealing and have plenty of flavour. If cooking outdoors, throw some sprigs of rosemary or bay leaves onto the coals or griddle for an instant, heady aroma.

To grow herbs successfully first prepare the container. Start by cleaning it; if it has been used for other plants remove all the old compost and scrub the pot out thoroughly with disinfectant to minimize the chance of any infection reaching the young plants. Herbs need excellent drainage, so fill the bottom of the pot with stones and broken pot or tiles. If planting a window box or wall-mounted planter, use bits of polystyrene packing material instead as they are so much lighter. Mix some horticultural sharp sand into the compost to aid drainage.

To help the herbs last from one year to the next, cut them back in the autumn so that next year's growth will be young and fresh. Regular clipping as you pick sprigs and leaves helps too. In winter, reduce watering, weed well and bring indoors the most tender (basil, for example, and even then this may not last the winter). Don't water outdoor herbs during the winter.

The following are among the easiest and most popular herbs for cooking:

- **Rosemary**
- **Thyme**
- **Bay**
- **Mint**
- **Parsley**
- **Chives**
- **Basil**
- **Sage**

outdoor cooking and heating

cooking

THE OBVIOUS cooker for cooking outdoors is of course the ubiquitous barbeque, and while there is nothing wrong with this popular gadget there are alternatives (see below). One thing holds true for them all, however. Food cooked outdoors tastes best if it is not taken straight from the refrigerator but has had time to reach room temperature first. You can also tenderize meat in advance with marinades, which will give it an especially delicious crust, as well as helping to keep it moist during cooking.

Alternatives to the traditional charcoal barbeque:

- Gas-powered barbeque
- Gas barbeque with self-cleaning lava-rock base (gives food a smoky flavour)
- Portuguese terracotta oven – low 'beehive' type
- Tall Mexican terracotta oven on wrought iron stand – looks magnificent even when not in use (see left)
- Portable gas-powered cooker with two rings
- Pit in the ground with a fire in it
- Wood or charcoal-fired stainless steel field cooker

eating

For eating outdoors, use your usual every-day china, or colourful and inexpensive china that won't cause heartache if it breaks, or use bright plastic picnic plates in different colours. Similarly if you're worried about breaking glasses, look at today's range of wine glasses and tumblers made in clear and coloured plastic and acrylic. There are beer mugs that can be pre-chilled in the freezer for a couple of hours, to keep drinks cool in the summer heat, and jugs that are either thermal or have a separate central well for ice, so that it doesn't dilute the drink when it melts.

heating

To heat your terrace or small garden in the cool of the evening, or during the day in late autumn or early spring, there are several options. One is to invest in a garden gas-powered heater. Alternatively, build a grate for an open fire or light a fire raised up in a brazier, with or without a lid to increase the spread of the heat.

THERE ARE many types of lighting available to illuminate the terrace and garden after dark, but the first question to ask is, what exactly do you want lit? To make the garden seem large, light upwards into trees and outwards to the boundaries. For an intimate feel, use candles and lamps on the table. For a dramatic, festive atmosphere, place flares and candles in the flowerbeds. In all cases, always be aware of the fire hazards.

Here are some ideas for candles and other live flames outdoors:

- **On a completely still evening, candlesticks on the table**
- **To protect the flame from breezes, use a glass storm lantern (available in various designs from traditional to sleek contemporary) or simple jam jars for tea lights**
- **Jam jars containing small candles or tea lights can be hung from trees. Simply cut a piece of wire four times the circumference of the jar, wind this twice around under the rim then create a hoop over the top for hanging, and secure**
- **Jam jars can be decorated with enamel and oil-based paints in gold, silver and translucent colours**
- **Citronella-scented candles give a zinging citrus aroma to the air, and repel bugs**
- **Canisters on split bamboo poles give a continuous renewable flare for hours on end. Fill the can with liquid paraffin and trim the wick**
- **A one-off flare is a type of candle on a stick which is pushed into the ground. A flower bed is a good location (but not where it could set fire to plants)**
- **Make your own 'flares' or garden candlesticks with pieces of copper (or other metal) piping, cut into varying lengths. Press a candle down into one end and push the other into the ground.**

Electric lighting can also work well in the garden, either wired permanently under the ground (get a professional to install this) or run out from the house for the occasion via heavy-duty cable. Be aware of the dangers of using electricity in damp places; keep cables and lamps away from ponds and from anything sharp that might cut the wiring. Solar-powered lights eliminate the need for wires or cables. Tuck them among plants, along the edges of beds or borders, or in containers. Finally, fairy lights look magical strung into trees in summer or winter.

outdoor
lighting

CHAPTER SEVEN

FOOD AND DRINK

'KITCHEN LIVING' FOOD IS FOR SHARING. IT IS SIMPLE AND A PLEASURE TO COOK, OFFERS DAZZLING FLAVOURS AND WONDERFUL SCENTS, AND LOOKS ENTICING, TOO. IT DRAWS INSPIRATION FROM THE CUISINE OF MANY COUNTRIES, INCLUDING THOSE OF THE MEDITERRANEAN, ASIA AND THE MIDDLE EAST. YOU MAY HAVE A HECTIC CAREER, YOU MAY HAVE CHILDREN… EITHER WAY YOU STILL WANT TO SPEND TIME ENJOYING FOOD WITH FRIENDS AND FAMILY, NOT DOING FIDDLY THINGS WITH KIWI FRUIT OR SLAVING OVER THE COOKER FOR HOURS ON END. COOKING AND EATING ARE SOCIAL, SENSORY EXPERIENCES, NOT SOME FORM OF COMPETITION. THE FOLLOWING PAGES REFLECT THIS RELAXED, INFORMAL APPROACH.

THIS CHAPTER dips into aspects of eating and drinking in the kitchen. It gives a handful of recipes for each course of a meal, from nibbles and first courses to main courses and puddings, and useful hints for choosing and serving cheese. This is food for people who get hungry and like to eat. Quantities are generous, dishes are packed with flavour and nothing takes long to prepare.

Finally, there are some fruity, alcohol-free concoctions for drinking in summer or winter (you can add a tot here and there for additional kick) and a choice of delicious infusions and tisanes, as well as instructions for making the perfect cup of tea.

This last chapter of Kitchen Living underlines the living kitchen lifestyle. This is not a cook book – it's a book for a way of life.

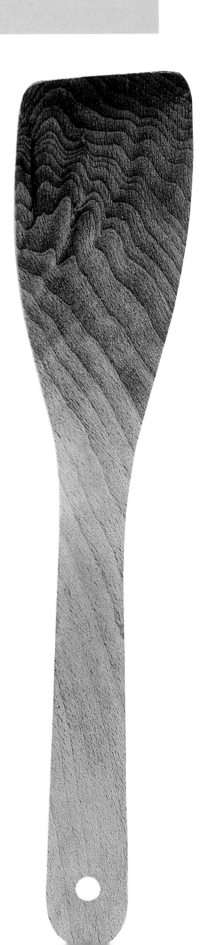

nibbles and first courses

oriental dumpling soup

This versatile soup is sufficiently delicate and exotic to serve as a first course at a dinner party, yet robust enough to be a lunch or supper dish on its own. Serves 8 as a first course and 4 to 6 as a meal in itself.

2.5 cm (1 in) piece root ginger, peeled

4 cloves garlic, peeled

Big handful fresh coriander leaves and stalks, well washed

Chicken thigh meat or lean pork (cut up into chunks) and prawns: any proportion to total 450 g (1 lb)

Juice of ½ a lime

1 egg white

Salt

1.7 litres (3 pints) chicken stock

3 medium carrots, topped, tailed and sliced into 5 cm (2 in) sticks

Bunch spring onions, prepared, cut into 5 cm (2 in) lengths, the white cut in two lengthways

3 bulbs pak choi or a bulb of Chinese leaves or a lettuce, coarsely sliced

1. Mince the ginger and garlic in a food processor.
2. Add the coriander, then the meat and prawns, then the lime juice and egg white and a good pinch of salt, and whizz again briefly.
3. Form this dumpling mixture into balls, a teaspoonful at a time. Because the mixture is sticky, it is easier to use two teaspoons (and this method makes neater, firmer balls) instead of your fingers.
4. Heat the stock in a wide pan until it boils then add the carrots.
5. After a couple of minutes, add the spring onions, then the bulbs of the pak choi, then the leaves.
6. When the mixture returns to the boil turn it down to a simmer, then add the dumplings individually, so that they don't stick together.
7. Turn off the heat after 30 seconds of simmering and serve immediately in soup plates as a starter or generous pasta bowls as a main course.

pepper pâté

Serves 4 as a first course, 2 as a lunch or supper dish. It can also be served on bread as a canapé or used as a pasta sauce (make plenty). This pâté tastes even better after a day kept in the fridge or a cool place.

2 tablespoons extra virgin olive oil

2 red, 1 yellow and 1 orange pepper cored, deseeded and cut into 2.5 cm (1 in) squares)

4 large cloves garlic, peeled (use more/less if preferred)

Salt and freshly ground black pepper

Handful fresh basil leaves

1. Heat the oil in a pan over a medium/low heat and gently fry the pepper pieces and garlic cloves until completely soft but not browned.
2. Allow to cool, add the basil leaves and mince in the food processor.
3. Taste and season (it may need lots of salt and pepper).
4. For a really rich, pungent flavour, add another clove of garlic, raw but peeled and finely minced.

onion bhajis

These little patties are infinitely variable. They can be made with other vegetables such as potato or aubergine, with extra chilli, or none, with or without fennel seeds, according to taste. They can be served hot, cold or warm, are an asset on picnics or long journeys and freeze well.

This quantity will make a starter for 4, a lunch or supper dish for 2 or nibbles for 8 people. Serve with a bowl of plain live yoghurt for dipping, or with a green or tomato salad and wedges of lemon for a lunch or supper dish.

175 g (6 oz) gram (chickpea) flour

3 tablespoons plain live yoghurt

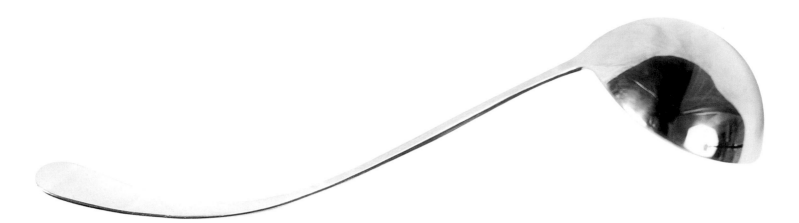

Cold water in a jug

2.5 cm (1 in) piece of root ginger (no need to peel it)

4 cloves garlic, peeled

Bunch fresh coriander with the roots cut off, well washed

1 dessertspoon fennel seeds

1 fresh red chilli

1 fresh green chilli

Salt

4 onions, peeled, quartered and sliced

275 ml (¹/₂ pint) sunflower oil for cooking

1. Put the flour and yoghurt in a large mixing bowl.

2. Stir together and add water a little at a time from the jug, until the mixture has the consistency of thick cream (if you add too much water, compensate with a bit more flour). Don't worry about lumps.

3. Leave this batter to stand for half an hour.

4. Mince the ginger, garlic, coriander and chillies (take off the tops but don't discard the seeds) in a food processor.

5. When the batter has stood, add the ginger mixture, the fennel seeds and the onions.

6. Heat the oil in a pan until very hot, then remove a tablespoon of the hot oil and add it to the batter, stirring it in.

7. Drop spoonfuls of the onion batter mixture into the pan and fry on both sides until brown (it may be necessary to add more oil). Drain on sheets of kitchen paper.

bean purée with rosemary oil

This freezes well so make plenty. If fact, having opened a bag of dried haricot or cannelloni beans you might as well cook them all. This dish can also be made on the spur of the moment with tinned beans. The extra rosemary oil can be used in dressings or for cooking, and will keep for at least a week or two.

Dried white beans

570ml (1 pint) extra virgin olive oil

Sprigs of rosemary

Onions

Bay leaves

Garlic

Salt and freshly ground black pepper

Ciabatta or other good white bread

1. Soak the beans overnight or for 24 hours.

2. Make the rosemary oil. Warm the oil in a small pan and plunge in the sprigs of rosemary, bruising the leaves with a wooden spoon. Cool then strain into a glass bottle with a fresh sprig of rosemary.

3. Drain the beans, cover with plenty of fresh, cold water, add quartered (not peeled) onions and some bay leaves but no salt and bring to the boil.

4. Boil hard for 10 minutes, skim any scum or froth and then simmer hard for 1¹/₂ hours or until really soft.

5. Drain the beans, remove the onions and bay leaves.

6. Mince the garlic in a food processor – as many cloves as you like, or none if you don't like raw garlic.

7. Add the beans to the bowl of the food processor and purée, pouring the rosemary oil slowly through the feeder tube as the blade turns. Continue until the purée is light, loose and glossy but not runny (you won't need anything like the whole pint of oil).

8. Taste and season with salt and pepper.

9. Serve with warmed ciabatta or toast.

main courses

pork with onions and plum jam

Effectively a form of sweet and sour pork, this dish is exceptionally quick and easy, its success depending upon the quality of the plum jam. Home-made is best, of course, so if you don't make plum jam yourself, seek out someone who does. The pork should be at room temperature before grilling, so that it cooks through evenly.

1 pork loin chop or leg steak per person

1 onion per chop, peeled, halved and sliced

2 tablespoons plum jam per chop

A little cold water

1. Preheat the grill to high.
2. Measure out the jam into a jug or bowl and mix with a dribble of cold water to loosen the consistency. If there are large plum pieces, cut these up with a pair of scissors.
3. Lie the chops in a shallow, fireproof dish.
4. Scatter the onions and spread the jam over.
5. Place under the grill and cook for about 15 minutes on the first side, 10 minutes on the second, until the pork is cooked through. Baste regularly, moving the plum pieces and onion around. The sugar will make the onion blacken and caramelize in places – this is part of the dish's sticky appeal.
6. Serve with buttery mashed potato, new potatoes or rice, and a green vegetable or salad.

seared squid

This is a simple dish, once you have prepared the squid. It is good with chilli oil or fried with cloves of peeled, coarsely chopped garlic added to the frying pan just before the squid. It can be served on its own with lemon wedges as a starter, or as a lunch or supper dish with warmed, crusty bread or basmati rice.

Butter or olive oil for frying (as much as required, depending on whether you want lots of oily/buttery sauce with the squid)

450 g (1 lb) small squid per person for lunch or supper

(half this amount for a first course and less per person if serving the squid on cocktail sticks as a nibble with chilli oil for dipping)

Optional chilli oil or chopped garlic cloves

1. Prepare the squid:

   Tip into a basin or sink of cold water and swill about. Pick a squid, grasp the sac in one hand and the tentacles in the other and pull apart, firmly but gently. Squeeze the sac to ensure all the soft bits are out (discard these), then pull out the long, clear, plastic-looking cartilage and discard. Set aside the sac. With a pair of scissors, cut off the entire bunch of tentacles, just below the eyes. Add the tentacle bunch to the sac and discard the rest. Repeat for the rest of the squid.

2. Cut the sacs into rings if you want.
3. Heat the oil or butter in a frying pan, and when hot, add the squid.
4. Cook for a short time, turning the squid over and over – for barely a minute or 2 (depending on the quantity) until all the pieces are opaque – and serve on hot plates.

fragrant fish (or chicken)

This dish is exceptionally pretty, with its red, yellow and green elements. It has the most enticing aroma, and can be made as mild or as spicy as you like. Feeds 4 with rice and perhaps a green salad.

With the addition of the extra fish and shellfish this dish will feed 4 for a feast or 6 for lunch.

Tomato sauce made (ideally) the previous day by frying 2 peeled and chopped onions and 4 peeled and chopped cloves of garlic in two tablespoons of olive oil, then adding dried herbs and an 800g tin of tomatoes. Simmer for a couple of hours (or more) and leave overnight

1 tablespoon good extra virgin olive oil

2.5 cm (1 in) piece root ginger chopped finely or grated

1 (or more) fresh green chilli(es), topped and sliced (don't discard seeds)

2 (or more) cloves garlic, peeled and roughly chopped

1 red and 1 yellow or orange pepper, cored, deseeded and sliced into long wedges

100 g creamed coconut, dissolved in 130 ml (5 fl oz) boiling water

Squirt of tomato purée

Few dashes Thai fish sauce

2 tablespoons ground almonds

Juice of 1/2 a lime or lemon (or more)

Salt

450 g (1 lb) small squid, prepared and the sacs cut into rings, and 450 g (1 lb) cod cut into 2.5 cm (1 in) pieces, or 700 g (1 1/2 lbs) chicken thigh meat, fat removed, cut into pieces

Bunch spring onions, topped and tailed and cut into 5 cm (2 in) lengths, the white split lengthways

Bunch fresh coriander leaves and stalks, well washed and shredded

1. Heat the oil in a casserole to medium/hot.
2. Fry the ginger and chillies, then after a couple of minutes add the garlic and peppers and turn them over in the heat a few times.
3. Add the dissolved creamed coconut, tomato sauce, purée, fish sauce, ground almonds and lime or lemon juice.

4. Bring to a simmer and stir. Add the fish or chicken, then the spring onions, and finally the coriander. Stir to heat through. The fish needs almost no time (approximately 1-2 minutes) before it is cooked, while chicken needs longer, (approximately 6-8 minutes)

onion tart

Another versatile dish, equally good served cold, warm or hot and creamy with steaming vegetables or a cold salad. When cold it firms up – so don't cook it too long or it will seem dry when cool. This pastry recipe is invaluable as it doesn't have to be cooked blind in advance.

For the pastry:

150 g (5 oz) self-raising flour

25 g (1 oz) grated Cheddar cheese

50 g (2 oz) butter

Level teaspoon English mustard powder

1 egg

For the filling:

4 onions, halved and sliced

25 g (1 oz) butter

6 large free-range eggs

Any of: plain live yoghurt, crème fraîche or double cream to make up the eggs to 570 ml (1 pint)

One tablespoon oil or 10 g (1/2 oz) butter for frying

Salt and freshly ground black pepper

25 g (1 oz) grated Cheddar cheese for the topping

1. Heat 25 g (1 oz) of butter in a frying pan and when hot add the onions, frying long and slow until they are soft and golden.
2. Make the pastry. Put all the ingredients into a food processor and run the blade until the mixture turns into a ball. Tip onto a plate and chill.
3. Heat the oven to 190°C/375°F/Gas Mark 5.
4. Blend all the filling ingredients, except onions ideally in a tall jug with a hand-held electric whisk or blender for convenience.
5. Prepare a deep, fluted (looks best, but not essential) 23 cm (9 in) metal flan dish with a loose bottom by first brushing it with melted butter then dusting this with flour.
6. Roll out the pastry on a floured surface and press loosely into the flan dish.
7. Spread the soft and golden onions evenly over the base then pour on the filling mixture. Sprinkle the topping cheese evenly.
8. Bake on a shelf in the middle of the oven for 35 minutes.
9. Allow to cool on a rack for a couple of minutes before loosening and removing the flan dish. Cool further (if required) on the rack before serving.

puddings and

pecan pie

For lovers of nuts, especially nuts in a sticky, toffee-like sauce encased in pastry, this version of the classic sweet tart is made with the same wonderful pastry recipe as the onion tart (see page 151) – it doesn't need baking blind and can be adapted to almost any dish. Leave out the cheese and add an extra 25g (1oz) butter. For a sweeter pastry (but don't forget how sweet the filling is), replace 25 g (1 oz) of the flour with white castor or fine brown sugar.

For the sauce:

150 g (5 oz) self-raising flour

Pinch of salt

75 g (3 oz) butter

1 egg

For the filling:

110 g (4 oz) melted butter

4 tablespoons maple syrup

75 g (3 oz) dark brown sugar

3 tablespoons double cream

1 teaspoon vanilla essence

350 g (12 oz) pecan nuts

1. Preheat the oven to 180°C/375°F/Gas Mark 4
2. Put the pastry ingredients in a food processor and whizz until the pastry has formed a ball.
3. Tip onto a plate and cool.
4. Prepare a 28 cm (11 in) shallow flan tin with a loose bottom by first brushing it with melted butter then dusting it with flour.
5. Put all the filling ingredients except the nuts into a jug and blend, ideally with a hand-held electric whisk or blender.
6. Roll out the pastry on a floured board and press gently into the flan dish.
7. Lay the nuts out on the pastry and gently pour over the filling mixture (if you do this too fast the nuts will shoot to one side).
8. Bake for around 25 minutes or until golden brown and serve with Greek yoghurt, cream or ice cream.

grilled mango

What can be more delicious than ripe fruit, especially mango, especially honey mango, seared by the heat of the grill, its flavour heightened by dark muscovado sugar and the zing of squeezed lime juice?

Mangoes (at least half per person)

Muscovado or other dark brown sugar to sprinkle over

Juice of ¹/₂ a lime (at least) per mango

1. Preheat the grill to high.
2. Halve the mangoes, removing the stones, score the flesh lengthways and widthways and turn inside out so the squares of flesh stand proud of the skin.
3. Scatter sugar over these and place under the grill until the sugar melts and the mango begins to singe.
4. Squeeze over the lime juice and serve.

cheeses

AS ENTERTAINING becomes more relaxed, the cheese board has come into its own; often an invitation to lunch or supper with friends will mean a main course followed simply by cheese and fruit.

The secret of an interesting cheese course is choice and presentation. Here are some valuable tips on both.

choosing cheeses:

- Don't serve too many pieces – three or four larger chunks are better than lots of little bits
- Have some variety – not all runny continental cheeses or firm British ones – and perhaps include a goat's or sheep's milk cheese
- Include at least one locally produced cheese if possible
- Cheeses should be in peak condition, ripe if they are soft. Test ripeness by pressing the centre of the cheese gently with your thumb. It should give but be springy
- If you can't find a fine herb and garlic soft cheese, make your own by mixing minced garlic (optional) and fresh herbs with a bought-in soft cheese and perhaps adding a little salt and pepper. Or roll balls of cream or curd cheese in different coloured crushed peppercorns or chopped fresh herbs.

presenting and serving cheeses:

- Have a decent-sized cheese board
- Make sure it is really clean. Ideally, keep a board specifically for cheeses, ie not one that is also used as a chopping board
- Make sure the knife is sharp enough
- Take the cheeses out of the fridge in good time for them to reach room temperature before serving
- Lay a bunch of grapes on the board with the cheeses, or a pile of fresh berries (in a small bowl, if they tend to move around or are too juicy)
- Serve a jar of celery alongside, or a plain green salad with a walnut oil dressing, if the meal has not included salad already
- Offer a variety of biscuits and/or breads
- At larger occasions, have two or more smaller dishes of butter rather than one large one which will take longer to circulate around the table.

fruit drinks

THERE ARE occasions when those who are not drinking alcohol seem to miss out… but not if they are enjoying one of the following fruity drinks. These concoctions are so delicious that the alcohol drinkers may want to hijack them for their own purposes. Simply add a tot of gin to the ones made with vegetable juice, or white rum to those with only fruit, with the exception of the lemon barley water. This is a classic summer thirst-quencher, ideal refreshment during games of tennis or croquet or after a walk or swim in the sun. As well as a blender or food processor, a juicer is essential for producing truly irresistible non-alcoholic drinks. Check that the model is easy to dismantle and clean before buying it.

firecracker

This is strong – an alternative to a Bloody Mary if you don't want alcohol and like the garlic. By all means leave out the garlic if you prefer, but you'll be taking the fire out of the firecracker.

Handful of fresh basil leaves

1 clove garlic, peeled

1 stick celery (a second with leaves, optional)

3 tomatoes, quartered

Generous pinch of salt

1. Put the basil leaves into the juicer first, then the garlic, then one stick of the celery.
2. Finally put the tomatoes and salt through the juicer. The tomatoes will help force the rest through.
3. Serve with the stick of celery with the leaves.

carrot cooler

This refreshing drink is as good before breakfast as it is drunk as an aperitif later in the day.

Handful of fresh coriander leaves and stalks

3 medium carrots

Juice of 2 oranges

1. Put the coriander leaves through the juicer first, then the carrots.
2. Add the orange juice and stir.

summer pudding

This is as good as the real pudding, and much less work. Mixed red berries can be bought ready-frozen if fresh are not available.

8 tablespoons of frozen red berries

275 ml (¹/₂ pint) good quality apple juice

Dash of cream

1. Whizz the berries in the blender.
2. Add the other ingredients and swirl.

minty melon

Handful of fresh mint leaves

¹/₄ Galia melon, deseeded, peeled and cut into cubes

Juice of a lime

1. Put the mint leaves through the juicer, followed by the melon.
2. Stir in the lime juice.

lemon barley water

4 tablespoons pearl barley

1.7 litres (3 pints) water

Juice of 2 lemons and 1 tablespoon sugar per pint of boiled liquid

1. Put the barley in a sieve and rinse it thoroughly under running water.
2. Put it in a pan with the water and bring to the boil.
3. Simmer the barley for at least 10 minutes and then strain it, retaining the liquid, initially in a measuring jug so you can see how much liquid is left after boiling. Discard the barley (or add it to soup or a casserole).
4. Allow the liquid to cool, then add the lemon juice and sugar and stir until dissolved.

infusions and tisanes

THERE'S NO better way of ending a meal, or the day, than with a hot drink. If you are sitting at table, or round the fire, it's an excuse to linger pleasurably, hands warm, feeling mellow, chatting about life and the world. It will help your digestion as well as your mood.

A hot drink is also the best thing to return to after a brisk walk on a winter's morning. Steaming tea or a hot whisky toddy warms the heart as well as the hands and the digestion. It adds both to your sense of well-being after exercise, and also to the welcome home.

hot whisky toddy

Cut a slice of lemon and stud the rind with several dried cloves. Place in a mug or sturdy glass tumbler with a measure of Irish whiskey or Scotch, and sugar to taste – a couple of teaspoons is usually sufficient. If making the toddy in a glass, leave the spoon in to help prevent it cracking when the water is added. Boil the water and let it go off the boil, then pour onto the spirit and leave to infuse for several minutes, or as long as you can resist, before drinking.

green tea

This is tea which was not fermented when manufactured. Consequently it has a light colour and flavour compared to black, or fermented, tea. Use only a pinch of leaf in a small pot at first – too much and the flavour becomes bitter. Adjust the amount of leaf to your taste with experience. Leave to infuse for five minutes or so, then, as with jasmine tea, drink from small cups without handles, or from a cup or mug in the Western style.

mint tea and herbal infusions

Herbs like mint and lemon balm make delicious infusions which can either be drunk immediately, hot, or allowed to cool and served chilled, with sprigs of fresh herb, as a summery drink. Mint stimulates the digestion, as does lemon balm, which is also an anti-depressant and is anti-bacterial. Boil fresh water but allow it to settle before pouring over fresh or dried herbs – 25 g (1 oz) of dried for 500 ml (approximately 1 pint) – three or four sprigs for a mug of infusion made from fresh herbs. Leave to stand and steep for ten minutes, by which time it will still be hot but cool enough to drink.

traditional tea

Warm the pot. Use an amount of leaves appropriate to the size of the pot, not the number of people drinking from it. Boil water fresh from the tap and allow it to boil thoroughly, not simply to reach boiling point. Pour over the leaves immediately and leave to infuse for six minutes. Any less and you won't get the true character of the tea coming through in a rich, dark liquor. In terms of flavour, it doesn't matter whether you add the milk first or afterwards. The advantages of adding it first are that the milk fat emulsifies better, and you don't need a spoon for stirring.

jasmine tea

This has similar qualities of lightness as green tea, but with the added attraction of the fragrance and flavour of jasmine flowers. Only a little leaf is needed to produce a golden colour and fine flavour – use no more than a pinch at first, until you establish the amount that suits your taste. After infusing in a pot for five or six minutes (no more), pour without straining if you like to see jasmine flowers floating in the cup.

acknowledgements

author's acknowledgements:

With grateful thanks to Clare Blackledge; Eugenie Boyd; Felicity Bryan; Kyle Cathie; Shân Dixon; Heather and David Hilliard; James Hodgson; Mr and Mrs David Hudd; Sue Jamieson; Georg Jensen; Andrie Morris; Sue and Richard Mosley; Mr and Mrs Norman North; Kate Oldfield; William Selka; Cathy Steele; The Stainless Steel Appeal; Peter Ting at Thomas Goode & Co; Rebecca Willis and Nick Ritblat.

publisher's acknowledgements:

We would like to thank the following for their enthusiastic contributions to this book: Heidi Baker; Marion Cotterall; Tasha Goddard; Mick and Gill Hodson; Antonia and Lucy Howatson; Nigella Lawson; Patrick Stockley; Abigail Ahern and Sally Conran at Wells Associates.

We would also like to thank the following for supplying props for photoshoots and/or images: Attenborough Associates; Camron Public Relations; Condor Public Relations; Adam Rubens at Fiesta Heaters; Grant Butler Coomber; Key Communications; Ali Kold; Lara Grylls PR; Leedex GTPR; Sofia Sommerskill; Publicity Engineers; Rennie Marketing and Communications; Rodney Saunders Associates; Sheila Fitzjones Public Relations; Sally MacDonald at The Conran Shop; The Ideas Network and Ware Anthony Rust.

Key:
CA   Caroline Arber
LH   Laura Hodgson
FY   Francesca Yorke

INTRODUCTION
page 1-3: CA; page 6: CA

PLANNING AND STORAGE
page 8: main picture, MFI Homeworks; bottom left, Corian; bottom middle, CA; bottom right, LH; page 10-11: LH; page 12: top, Fulham Kitchens; bottom, Shaker; page 13: Bulthaup; page 14: main picture, Smeg; top left, De Dietrich; middle, Smeg; bottom, Aga; page 15: top, Corian; bottom, Shaker; page 18: John Cullen Lighting; page19: clockwise from top left, Ikea; McCord; Ocean; McCord; page 20-21: CA; page 22: left, Shaker; right, CA; page 23: top, CA; bottom, G.E.C. Anderson; page 24: CA; page 25: left, LH; right, CA; page 27: main picture and bottom right, Newcastle Furniture Company; top right, CA; middle, Smallbone of Devizes; page 28: FY; page 29: Bulthaup; page 30-31: FY; page 34: Kirkstone; page 35: Space Savers; page 36-43: CA; page 45: De Dietrich; page 46-47: Whirlpool; page 48-49: Chalon

DECORATING THE KITCHEN
page 50: Ray Main/Mainstream/Plain and Simple Kitchens; page 52: top, Aga; bottom, Ray Main/Mainstream/Plain and Simple Kitchens; page 53: top left, Roundhouse; top right and bottom left, G.E.C. Anderson; bottom right, CA; page 54: Ray Main/Mainstream; page 57: clockwise from left, G.E.C. Anderson; Kenneth Clark Ceramics; Shaker; LH; page 58: clockwise from left, Dalsouple; Sinclair Till; Lassco; Paris Ceramics; page 59: Amtico; page 61: clockwise from left, BLU; Fourneaux de France; Shaker; Kirkstone; Corian; Kirkstone; page 62: Kiosk; page 63: top right, Kiosk; bottom left, CA; bottom right, Amtico; page 64-5: Ray Main/Mainstream; page 67: Milo Design; page 68: Superstock; page 70: top right, Harvey Jones; bottom right, Bulthaup; page 71: Ocean; page 72: Bulthaup; page 73: top, Wireworks; bottom, Rhode Design

TABLES AND CHAIRS
page 74: CA; page 76: LH; page 77: top, Muji; bottom, Shaker; page 78-79: Table Makers; page 80: Multiyork; page 83: right, Multiyork; left, The Chair Company; page 84: top left and bottom right, Viaduct; top right, Muji; bottom left, The Chair Company; page 86: Purves and Purves; page 87: CA

FINISHING TOUCHES
page 88: CA; page 90: main picture, La Murina; left, CA; page 91: right, CA; page 92-95: CA; page 96: main picture, Fulham Kitchens; top, Shaker;

useful contacts

bottom, CA; page 97: bottom left, CA; bottom right, Bulthaup; page 98: Fired Earth; page 100: McCord; page 101: clockwise from left, LH; McCord; FY; FY; McCord; page 102: left, Nolte; right, CA; page 103: FY; page 104-105: Eclectics; page 106: Laura Ashley; page 108-109: CA; page 110-111: CA; page 112-113: CA

THE TABLE
page 114: CA; page 116: CA; page 117: FY; page 118-119: CA; page 120: Plain English; page 121: CA; page 122-123: FY; page 124-125: CA; page 126-127: CA; page 128: LH; page 130-131: CA; page 132-133: CA

THE TERRACE
page 134: LH; page 135: FY; page 136-137: Garden Matters/John Feltwell; page 138-139: LH; page 140-141: LH; page 142-143: FY; page 144: Iguana; page 145: Fiesta Heaters

FOOD AND DRINK
page 146-147: LH; page 149-153: LH; page 154-155: CA

The publishers have endeavoured to get permission to reproduce all the photographs in this publication. If we have unwittingly overlooked any, we sincerely apologise and will be pleased to rectify the situation in all forthcoming editions.

Dalsouple
stockist details: 01984 667551

Eclectics
stockist details: 0870 0102211

Fiesta Heaters
Sovereign House
34 Robeson Way
Borehamwood
Hertfordshire WD6 5RY
020 8386 5122

Georg Jensen
14 Sloane Street
London SW1X 9NB
020 7235 0331

Harvey Jones
0800 9172340

La Murina
79 Ebury Street
London SW1W 0NZ
020 7730 7922

Purves and Purves
80-81 Tottenham Court Road
London W1P 9HD
020 7580 8223

Rhode Design
020 7354 9933

Selfridges
400 Oxford Street
London W1A 1AB
020 7629 1234

Shaker
72-73 Marylebone High Street
London W1M 3AR
020 7935 9461

Smallbone & Co.
105-109 Fulham Road
London SW3 6RL
020 7581 9989

Space Boudoir
214 Westbourne Grove
London W11 2RH
020 7229 6533

Space Savers
222 Kentish Town Road
London NW5 2AD
020 7485 3266

Stuart Crystal
mail order: 0500 101045

Table Makers
149 St Johns Hill
London SW11 1TQ
020 7223 2075

The Chair Company
82 Parsons Green Lane
London SW6 4HU
020 736 5478

The Conran Shop
81 Fulham Road
London SW3 6RD
020 7589 7401

Viaduct Furniture
1-10 Summer's Street
London EC1R 5BD
020 7278 2844

Whirlpool UK
stockist details: 0870 600 898

Wireworks
131a Broadley Street
London NW8 8BA
020 7724 8856

Zanussi
stockist details: 0870 5727727

index